SPANISH

SHORT
STORIES
FOR
BEGINNERS

**Fun short stories that will expand
your understanding of Spanish**

Written by Juan García

Channel Reader

Table of Contents

Introduction

Congratulations on your recent commitment! You are now the owner of a fantastic set of short stories designed to help you speak, think and understand Spanish. Unlike many text books, these stories are designed to be fun. In order to best help you, a summary in both Spanish and English has been placed at the beginning of each story. This will give you context. Bold type words are defined periodically within the text and also at the end in a vocabulary list. Be sure to pay attention because there are questions after each story so you can check your comprehension. Answers can be found on the following page, but don't cheat! You will learn the most if you review each story at least three times before moving on.

I hope you enjoy this collection of short stories. A tremendous amount of effort went into its creation. If you like this book please do me a favor and leave a review.

UNA AVENTURA GOURMET
RESUMEN

Robert es un chico de veinticinco años quien, por satisfacer a sus padres, estudia algo que en realidad no le gusta. Al graduarse decide emprender su verdadero sueño, que es el de ser un chef internacional. Se embarca en una aventura a través de los diferentes restaurantes de la ciudad para así ampliar su paladar con los distintos platos que pruebe y decidirse por cuál de las ramas culinarias dedicar su carrera.

Robert is a 25-year-old boy who, in order to please his parents, studies something that he really doesn't like. After his graduation, he decides to undertake his true dream, which is to be an international chef. He embarks on an adventure through the different restaurants in the city to expand his palate with the different dishes he tries and decide which culinary branch to dedicate his career to.

UNA AVENTURA GOURMET

Robert es un **chico** de veinticinco **años de edad**, quien **vive** junto a sus dos **padres** en la **ciudad** de Maracaibo, **ubicada** en Venezuela, cuya profesión es **ingeniero mecánico** solo para **satisfacer** el deseo de su **papá** José, pero en su interior, Robert siempre quiso ser chef.

1. **Chico:** Boy
2. **Años de edad:** Years old
3. **Vive**: Lives
4. **Padres**: Parents
5. **Ciudad:** City
6. **Ubicada**: Located

7. **Ingeniero mecánico:** Mechanical engineer

8. **Satisfacer**: Satisfy

9. **Papá**: Dad

Días después de **graduarse** como ingeniero, él toma la **decisión** que quiere buscar y **perseguir** sus **sueños**.

Uno de ellos es ser un gran **chef** en su ciudad natal y si el **destino** así lo quiere, poder **representar** a su **país** en el extranjero.

10. **Días:** Days

11. **Graduarse:** Graduate

12. **Decisión:** Decision

13. **Perseguir:** Pursue

14. **Sueños:** Dreams

15. **Chef:** Chef

16. **Destino:** Destiny

17. **Representar:** Represent

18. **País:** Country

Una tarde de abril, se dispone a hacer su **currículo** y **pedir** los **numerosos cursos** que ha hecho correspondiente a la cocina nacional, salsas madres y **repostería**, entre otros.

Así mismo, se le viene la grandiosa **idea** que también tiene la opción de poder **trabajar** en el exterior debido a la cantidad de cursos de **platos internacionales**, como la cocina **francesa**, **mediterránea, italiana** y **asiática**.

19. **Currículo:** Curriculum

20. **Pedir:** Order

21. **Numerosos:** Numerous
22. **Cursos:** Courses
23. **Repostería:** Baking
24. **Idea:** Idea
25. **Trabajar:** To work
26. **Platos internacionales:** International dishes
27. **Francesa:** French
28. **Mediterránea:** Mediterranean
29. **Italiana:** Italian
30. **Asiática:** Asian

Robert, hace una **inmensa** lista de **restaurantes** que desea **visitar** para probar su **comida**, para así vivir en **experiencia** propia, los diversos **sabores** y gustos de cada **rincón** de la comida en su región y así mismo de la comida internacional, realizada por diferentes tipos de chefs.

El primero en su **lista**, es un restaurante español llamado «Olé», que se caracteriza por su **magnífico plato** de paella, realizada a la **vista** de los **clientes** en una enorme **sartén**.

31. **Inmensa:** Immense
32. **Restaurantes:** Restaurants
33. **Visitar:** To visit
34. **Comida:** Food
35. **Experiencia:** Experience
36. **Sabores:** Flavors
37. **Rincón:** Corner
38. **Lista:** List
39. **Magnífico:** Magnificent
40. **Plato:** Dish

41. **Vista:** View

42. **Clientes:** Customers

43. **Sartén:** Frying Pan

Robert decide ir solo al restaurante para concentrarse en los diferentes sabores del plato y así ir entrenando su paladar.

Robert, al acercarse al restaurante, inmediatamente el mesero lo saluda y dice:

—Hola. ¿Cómo está esta tarde?

—Muy bien, gracias —responde Robert—. Quisiera probar la comida de aquí, ya que he leído muchas **reseñas** excelentes acerca del lugar, en la revista **culinaria** de la ciudad.

—**Perfecto**, no se va a arrepentir, ¿**mesa** para uno? —dice el mesero.

—Sí, esta vez solo seré yo. ¿Puedo ver el **menú**, por favor? —pregunta Robert.

—Claro, aquí lo tiene. Mientras usted decide, voy a atender a los otros **comensales** —dice el mesero.

Robert estudia de forma cuidadosa el menú. Indeciso acerca de cual plato **pedir**, decide llamar de nuevo al **mesero** y preguntarle:

44. **Reseñas:** Reviews

45. **Culinaria:** Culinary

46. **Perfecto:** Perfect

47. **Mesa:** Table

48. **Menú:** Menu

49. **Comensales:** Diners

50. **Pedir:** Order

51. **Mesero:** Waiter

—¿Cuál es el plato **especial** para el día de hoy?

Orgulloso responde el mesero:

—Nuestro plato especial es siempre la paella, que es la especialidad de nuestro chef, pero siempre podemos ofrecer otros **platos típicos** de España.

Robert responde **emocionado**:

52. **Especial:** Special
53. **Platos típicos:** Typical dishes
54. **Emocionado:** Excited

—¡Excelente!, me parece perfecto. Quisiera pedir la Paella.

—Seguro, ¿quieres algo de **beber**? —dice el mesero.

—Sí, me gustaría tomar una copa de vino. Y para cuando llegue la comida, quisiera un **jugo de fresa,** por favor.

El mesero responde:

—**Gracias**, en breve le traigo su plato.

55. **Beber:** To drink
56. **Jugo de fresa:** Strawberry juice,
57. **Gracias:** Thank you

Veinticinco minutos después llega el mesero...

—Aquí tiene, señor. Que disfrute su comida.

Robert responde:

—Gracias.

Una vez servido el plato en la mesa, Robert comienza a **degustarlo**, sintiendo todos los sabores característicos de la cocina Española. Recordando las excelentes reseñas que había leído, se **sonríe** porque todo lo que leyó fue cierto y no se arrepiente.

58. **Degustarlo:** Taste it
59. **Sonríe:** Smile

Una vez terminado su plato, se acerca el mesero diciendo:

—¿Puedo ofrecerle algo más?

—No, gracias. Estoy satisfecho así, la paella me llenó por completo. Me gustaría la cuenta, por favor —responde Robert.

—Seguro, son $14.95 —dice el mesero.

—Aquí tiene. Por favor, quédese con el cambio por su excelente **atención** —dice Robert.

—¡Muchas gracias, señor! Por lo que veo, no está **arrepentido** de nuestro plato especial. Lo esperaremos pronto, ¡que tenga un excelente día!

Robert responde:

—Gracias a usted, no me arrepentí, por el contrario, me encantó la **explosión** de sabores de esa paella. De seguro voy a regresar. Adiós.

Robert, emocionado, regresa a su casa, para hacer las respectivas **anotaciones** acerca del restaurante que visitó, entre ellas, escribe los **ingredientes** que pudo saborear para así intentar **rehacer** una paella y poder darle su **toque personal**.

60. **Atención:** Attention
61. **Arrepentido:** Regretful
62. **Explosión:** Explosion
63. **Anotaciones:** Annotations
64. **Ingredientes:** Ingredients
65. **Rehacer:** Redo/Remake

66. **Toque personal:** Personal touch

Al **siguiente día**, Robert le comenta a sus dos amigos Elena y Luis acerca de lo que viene haciendo y les dice que el próximo restaurante en su lista es el llamado «Mamma mía», **especializado** en **comida italiana** que también tiene excelentes reseñas según los mejores críticos de la región.

Llegan al lugar, y piden una mesa para tres personas. El mesero los hace pasar para ubicarlos en su respectiva mesa, al lado de una **réplica** de la «Torre de Pisa» y debajo de un cuadro similar al de la «Creación de Adán», que es una famosa **pintura** ubicada en la Capilla Sixtina, localizada en el Vaticano, Italia.

67. **Siguiente día:** Next day
68. **Especializado:** Specialized
69. **Comida italiana:** Italian food
70. **Réplica:** Replica
71. **Pintura:** Painting

Todos se sientan y Robert le pregunta al mesero:

—¿Será que nos puede traer el menú, por favor?

El mesero se retira a buscarlo, mientras ellos aprecian los detalles del lugar.

Luis, leyendo el menú, pregunta a Robert:

—¿Has leído acerca de la especialidad de este restaurante?

Robert responde:

—Sí, hablan mucho acerca del **espagueti**, **pizzas** y **lasaña**, pero en general dicen que toda la comida es muy buena y vale la pena probarlo todo.

72. **Espagueti:** Spaghetti

73. **Pizzas:** Pizzas

74. **Lasaña:** Lasagna

Elena sugiere que cada uno pida un plato distinto para así probar gran variedad de su menú.

—¡Perfecto! —responden Robert y Luis al mismo tiempo. Se disponen a llamar al mesero para así pedir sus platos.

El mesero pregunta:

—¿Listos para pedir?

Robert se adelanta y responde:

—¡Sí!, yo voy a querer un espagueti con **salsa** a la boloñesa, para mi amigo Luis, le puede traer una pizza con pepperoni y para mi amiga Elena le trae una lasaña, eso es todo.

Luis **inmediatamente** llama al mesero de nuevo quien se estaba retirando y le dice:

—Disculpe, a mi amigo se le olvidó ordenar las bebidas, por favor nos va a traer tres limonadas, pero cuando lleguen los platos que pedimos.

El mesero responde entre risas nerviosas.

—Disculpe, a mí también se me **olvidó** preguntar qué iban a tomar. **Enseguida** le traigo sus pedidos, el tiempo de espera estimado es de treinta minutos.

Durante el tiempo de espera, Robert les contaba a sus amigos cuáles eran sus **planes** para el futuro, y que quería empezar una nueva vida en el mundo culinario, especializándose en comida internacional.

75. **Salsa:** Sauce

76. **Inmediatamente:** Immediately

77. **Se me olvidó:** I forgot

78. **Enseguida:** Right away/Straightaway

79. **Planes:** Plans

Minutos más tarde, llega la comida.

—Este espagueti está **increíble** —dice Luis.

Robert responde:

—La verdad que sí, amigo. ¿Qué tal la lasaña, Elena?

Elena responde:

—Está muy buena, pero creo que tu espagueti está mejor.

Robert propone:

—Hagamos algo, vamos a **intercambiar platos** y así todos podemos decidir cuál de los tres platos ha sido el mejor. ¿Les parece?

80. **Increíble:** Amazing
81. **Intercambiar platos:** Exchange dishes

Todos intercambian los diferentes platos y **concluyen** que el mejor fue el espagueti con salsa a la boloñesa, ya que el pepperoni de la pizza estaba un poco picante. Sin embargo, la lasaña se lleva el segundo lugar.

Robert comenta:

—Todo estaba muy bueno, a excepción del pepperoni, pero definitivamente volveré a venir.

El mesero se acerca y les pregunta:

—¿Quieren algún **postre**?

82. **Concluyen:** Conclude
83. **Postre:** Dessert

Elena dice:

—Sí, me trae una tarta de limón, por favor.

Luis dice entre risas:

—Yo estoy muy lleno, pero igual voy a probar esa tarta de limón.

Robert le dice al mesero:

—Yo voy a pedir unos cannolis. Y le comenta a sus amigos que son los dulces más conocidos de la ciudad de Sicilia en Italia, dato que aprendió en el curso de repostería italiana.

Minutos más tarde, luego de degustar los postres y estar de acuerdo que los cannolis eran el mejor postre que habían probado, deciden pedir la cuenta al mesero.

—Me trae la cuenta, por favor —dice Robert.

—Aquí la tiene, son $80,50 —dice el mesero.

Robert se levanta a **pagar** el total de la cuenta, ya que fue él quien invitó a sus amigos.

Robert llega a su casa para realizar las respectivas anotaciones de la visita a los restaurantes en su lista.

Se da cuenta que pudo **recorrer** la **mayoría** de los estilos de cocina que aprendió en los cursos realizados. Por lo cual decide que quiere especializarse en la comida italiana.

84. **Pagar:** Pay
85. **Se da cuenta:** He realizes
86. **Recorrer:** Cover
87. **Mayoría:** Most

Recordando aquel restaurante llamado «Mamma Mia» que fue a visitar con sus amigos Luis y Elena, busca sus anotaciones y lee al pie de la letra la receta que pudo escribir de los cannolis que degustó aquel día.

Realiza la receta una y otra vez hasta poder lograr hacerlos de la misma manera y con el mismo sabor de aquellos cannolis del restaurante italiano.

Tras varios intentos **fallidos**, Robert decide ir de nuevo al restaurante. Al llegar, busca al mismo mesero que lo atendió la ultima vez y le dice:

—He intentado realizar la receta de los famosos cannolis de este restaurante y no lo he **logrado**, vengo una vez más para probarlos y así dar con el punto **exacto** de su sabor.

88. **Tras:** After
89. **Fallidos:** Failed
90. **Logrado:** Accomplished
91. **Exacto:** Exact

El mesero riéndose, responde:

—Enseguida le traigo su pedido, si **logra** hacerlos iguales le aseguro que hablaré con mi jefe para que tenga un puesto en la cocina de este restaurante.

Después de esa vez, Robert llega a su casa **decidido** a realizarlos igual y se da cuenta que solo le falta un ingrediente para hacerlos a la perfección.

Al hacerlos, se da cuenta que son iguales a los del restaurante por lo cual corre enseguida para que los pruebe el mesero y cumpla con su palabra.

Al llegar, el mesero los prueba y exclama:

—¡Definitivamente voy a hablar con mi **jefe** para que lo **contratemos**!, ha logrado a la perfección una receta de años de mejoría. Felicidades.

Robert emocionado exclama que finalmente puede cumplir su sueño de ser chef de comida internacional italiana.

92. **Logra:** Manages to

93. **Decidido:** Determined

94. **Jefe:** Boss

95. **Contratemos:** Let's hire

UNA AVENTURA GOURMET
PREGUNTAS

1. **¿Qué es lo que realmente le gusta hacer a Robert?**

   a. Ser ingeniero mecánico

   b. Ser chef

   c. Ser crítico de comidas.

2. **¿Qué tipo de comida sirve el restaurante «Olé»?**

   a. Italiana

   b. Mediterránea

   c. Española

3. **¿Con quién va Robert al restaurante italiano?**

   a. Solo

   b. Con su papá

   c. Con sus dos amigos

4. **¿Qué plato ordena Elena?**

   a. Lasaña

   b. Pizza

   c. Espagueti

5. **¿En qué se quiere especializar Robert?**

   a. Repostería

   b. Comida internacional italiana

   c. Comida nacional

UNA AVENTURA GOURMET
SOLUCIONES

1. B

2. C

3. C

4. C

5. B

UNA AVENTURA GOURMET
VOCABULARIO

1. **Chico:** Boy
2. **Años de edad:** Year old
3. **Vive:** Lives
4. **Padres:** Parents
5. **Ciudad:** City
6. **Ubicada:** Located
7. **Ingeniero mecánico:** Mechanical engineer
8. **Satisfacer:** Satisfy
9. **Papá:** Dad
10. **Días:** Days
11. **Graduarse:** Graduate
12. **Decisión:** Decision
13. **Perseguir:** Pursue
14. **Sueños:** Dreams
15. **Chef:** Chef
16. **Destino:** Destiny
17. **Representar:** Represent
18. **País:** Country
19. **Currículo:** Curriculum
20. **Pedir:** Order
21. **Numerosos:** Numerous
22. **Cursos:** Courses
23. **Repostería:** Baking
24. **Idea:** Idea
25. **Trabajar:** To work
26. **Platos internacionales:** International dishes
27. **Francesa:** French
28. **Mediterránea:** Mediterranean
29. **Italiana:** Italian
30. **Asiática:** Asian
31. **Inmensa:** Immense
32. **Restaurantes:** Restaurants
33. **Visitar:** To visit
34. **Comida:** Food
35. **Experiencia:** Experience
36. **Sabores:** Flavors
37. **Rincón:** Corner
38. **Lista:** List
39. **Magnífico:** Magnificent
40. **Plato:** Dish
41. **Vista:** View
42. **Clientes:** Customers

43. **Sartén:** Frying Pan

44. **Reseñas:** Reviews

45. **Culinaria:** Culinary

46. **Perfecto:** Perfect

47. **Mesa:** Table

48. **Menú:** Menu

49. **Comensales:** Diners

50. **Mesero:** Waiter

51. **Especial:** Special

52. **Platos típicos:** Typical dishes

53. **Emocionado:** Excited

54. **Beber:** To drink

55. **Jugo de fresa:** Strawberry juice

56. **Gracias:** Thank you

57. **Degustarlo:** Taste it

58. **Sonríe:** Smile

59. **Atención:** Attention

60. **Arrepentido:** Regretful

61. **Explosión:** Explosion

62. **Anotaciones:** Annotations

63. **Ingredientes:** Ingredients

64. **Rehacer:** Redo/Remake

65. **Toque personal:** Personal touch

66. **Siguiente día:** Next day

67. **Especializado:** Specialized

68. **Comida italiana:** Italian food

69. **Réplica:** Replica

70. **Pintura:** Painting

71. **Espagueti:** Spaghetti

72. **Pizzas:** Pizzas

73. **Lasaña:** Lasagna

74. **Salsa:** Sauce

75. **Inmediatamente:** Immediately

76. **Se me olvidó:** I forgot

77. **Enseguida:** Right away/Straightaway

78. **Planes:** Plans

79. **Increíble:** Amazing

80. **Intercambiar platos:** Exchange dishes

81. **Concluyen:** Conclude

82. **Postre:** Dessert

83. **Pagar: To** pay

84. **Se da cuenta:** He realizes

85. **Recorrer:** Cover

86. **Mayoría:** Most

87. **Tras:** After

88. **Fallidos:** Failed

89. **Logrado:** Accomplished

90. **Exacto:** Exact

91. **Logra:** to manage to

92. **Decidido:** Determined

93. **Jefe:** Boss

94. **Contratemos:** Let's hire

UN VIAJE AL SUPERMERCADO
RESUMEN

Michael, un señor de treinta y dos años, junto a sus dos amigos Carlos y Pedro, trabajan como abogados. Al ganar un importante caso, Michael tiene la grandiosa idea de realizar un corto viaje de fin de semana a la playa para celebrar. Antes de viajar se disponen a realizar una lista con todo lo necesario para el viaje, incluyendo los alimentos que diariamente van a consumir. Para ello, se dirigen al supermercado más cercano para realizar la compra y así no pasar nada por alto.

Michael, a 32-year-old man, along with his friends Carlos and Pedro, work as lawyers. By winning an important case, Michael has the great idea of making a weekend trip to the beach to celebrate. Before traveling, they make a list with everything they need for the trip, including the food they will consume daily. For this, they go to the nearest supermarket to make the purchase and thus, not overlook anything.

UN VIAJE AL SUPERMERCADO

Una **tarde** de agosto, Michael un **hombre** de treinta y dos años que vive en Río de Janeiro, Brasil, tiene una gran idea de realizar un **corto viaje** de fin de semana con sus amigos del trabajo.

Carlos de veintiocho años y Pedro de treinta y un años, un par de **abogados** que junto a él, habían ganado un **importante** caso y como **premio** por haberlo logrado, deciden ir a la **playa**.

1.   **Tarde:** Afternoon

2. **Hombre:** Man

3. **Corto viaje:** Short trip

4. **Abogados:** Lawyers

5. **Importante:** Important

6. **Premio:** Reward

7. **Playa:** Beach

Con varios días de **anticipación** realizan una lista detallada de todo lo necesario para el corto viaje.

Desde la **ruta de carretera** que van a tomar, **alquilar** una casa cerca de la playa que van a visitar, que incluya una gran **parrillera**, hasta los **alimentos** que van a consumir **diariamente**, sin olvidar el gran **asado** de la primera noche y la ensalada de **mariscos** del último día del **paseo**.

8. **Anticipación:** Anticipation

9. **Ruta de carretera:** Road route

10. **Alquilar:** To rent

11. **Parrillera**: Barbecue

12. **Alimentos:** Food

13. **Diariamente:** Daily

14. **Asado:** Roast/Barbecue

15. **Mariscos:** Seafood

16. **Paseo:** Ride

El fin de semana previo a la fecha pautada para el viaje, Michael, Carlos y Pedro se reúnen en casa de Michael para disponerse a salir al **supermercado** más cercano.

De esta forma pueden realizar la **compra** de los alimentos necesarios para el menú que han elegido para el viaje.

Al llegar al supermercado deciden que lo primero que deben hacer es comprar todo lo **referente** a verduras.

Van a la sección de **comida fresca** y una linda **trabajadora** del área, llamada María amablemente les pregunta:

17. **Supermercado:** Supermarket
18. **Compra:** Purchase
19. **Referente:** Concerning
20. **Verduras:** Vegetables
21. **Comida fresca:** Fresh food
22. **Trabajadora:** Worker

—¿En qué los puedo ayudar?

—Estamos buscando verduras frescas para un viaje de fin de semana —responde Michael.

—¿Qué tipo de verduras **buscan**? Las tienen que elegir dependiendo del tipo de comida que tienen pensado hacer —dice María.

A lo que Carlos responde:

—Sí, eso es cierto amigos. Tenemos pensado hacer una **ensalada** fresca de diferentes tipos de **lechugas** para acompañar una parrilla.

—Perfecto, vengan por aquí donde están todas las **legumbres**, y como pueden ver están muy frescas —responde María.

Michael y Carlos, poco conocedores de la **elección** de las mejores verduras, le piden ayuda a Pedro para que él las elija, pero Pedro tampoco sabe mucho sobre eso.

23. **Buscan:** Search
24. **Ensalada:** Salad

25. **Lechugas:** Lettuce
26. **Legumbres:** Legumes
27. **Elección:** Selection

Al ver María su poca experiencia para elegir las verduras, entre risas dice:

—Se puede ver que tienen poca experiencia en la elección de verduras, yo los ayudo a **escoger**, para que así se lleven lo mejor de la **tienda**.

A lo que todos apenados y riéndose responden:

—Muchas gracias, María, no pudimos ocultar nuestra **inexperiencia**.

María se dispone a escoger de manera **detallada** cada tipo de lechuga que hay en el **mostrador** y al finalizar pregunta:

—¿**Necesitan** algo más?

Y Pedro exaltado responde:

—¡Oh, sí! Se me olvidaban los **ingredientes** de la ensalada de mariscos que voy a preparar para el último día del viaje. Los voy a sorprender con el fabuloso ceviche que me enseñó a **preparar** mi tía.

28. **Escoger:** To Choose
29. **Tienda:** Store
30. **Inexperiencia:** Inexperience
31. **Detallada:** Detailed
32. **Mostrador:** Counter
33. **Necesitan:** They need (verb: necesitar)
34. **Ingredientes:** Ingredients
35. **Preparar:** To prepare

—Para eso van a necesitar **cebolla**, **pimentón** y sobretodo unos muy buenos mariscos que están en nuestra sección de **productos del mar** —dice María.

Luego de escoger todas las verduras para ambas recetas, María lleva a Michael, Carlos y Pedro a la sección de productos del mar.

En esta sección, se encuentran con unos grandes **refrigeradores** llenos de diferentes especies de animales marinos **congelados**, listos para usar.

36. **Cebolla:** Onion
37. **Pimentón:** Paprika
38. **Productos del mar:** Products of the sea
39. **Refrigeradores:** Refrigerators
40. **Congelados:** Frozen

Michael, Carlos y Pedro con su cara de **asombro** por la gran **variedad** de productos del mar que tiene el supermercado, le dicen a María:

—Creo que también necesitamos que nos ayudes con la elección de los mariscos —dice Michael con cara de confundido.

—Sí, María, solo necesito un par de **gramos** de **camarones** frescos y otro par de gramos de **calamares** —dice Pedro, para así poder preparar la fabulosa **receta** de su tía.

41. **Asombro:** Amazement
42. **Variedad:** Variety
43. **Gramos:** Grams
44. **Camarones:** Shrimp
45. **Calamares:** Squids
46. **Receta:** Recipe

A lo que responde María:

—Con gusto los ayudo con la elección de los mariscos, todos nuestros clientes se sienten igual frente a estos **enormes** refrigeradores.

Al ya haber escogido los camarones y calamares del gran refrigerador, Michael, Carlos y Pedro se disponen a caminar por los **pasillos** restantes del supermercado para elegir los productos faltantes de su **lista**.

Al pasar por la **sección** de **carnes**, Michael, Carlos y Pedro piensan en lo necesario para realizar el asado que tienen pautado para la primera noche del viaje de fin de semana.

Al ver que no encuentran en ese supermercado lo que quieren para realizar la **parrilla**, Michael dice:

—Es mejor que compremos la carne para el asado en otro lugar.

—Sí, veo que no te gusta el tipo de carne de este supermercado, conozco una carnicería cerca de mi casa donde la carne es de muy buena **calidad** —dice Pedro.

47. **Enormes:** Huge
48. **Pasillos:** Corridors
49. **Lista:** List
50. **Sección:** Section
51. **Carnes:** Meats
52. **Parrilla:** Grill
53. **Calidad:** Quality

—Paguemos esto, para así ir a la **carnicería** que dice Pedro —responde Carlos.

Al llegar a la **caja registradora** para **pagar** todo lo que eligieron en el supermercado, se despiden de María y agradecen su excelente **atención**, a lo que María responde entre risas:

—Espero verlos de nuevo muy **pronto**, y así enseñarles un poco más sobre la elección de verduras y mariscos.

Al salir del supermercado, Michael, Carlos y Pedro se suben al **carro** y se disponen a ir por la ruta más cercana.

De esta forma llegan lo más **rápido** posible a la carnicería cerca de la casa de Pedro, ya que se acercaba la hora de su **cierre**.

54. **Carnicería:** Butcher shop
55. **Caja registradora:** Cash register
56. **Pagar:** To pay
57. **Atención:** Attention
58. **Pronto:** Soon
59. **Carro:** Car
60. **Rápido:** Fast
61. **Cierre:** Closing

En el camino hacia la carnicería, los tres amigos **repasan** una y otra vez la lista de alimentos que hicieron para el viaje.

Se dan cuenta que no anotaron algo muy **importante**, las **bebidas**. Por lo que Michael exclama:

—Creo que tenemos que **volver** al supermercado, nos **olvidamos** de colocar en la lista las diferentes bebidas que necesitamos para poder pasar el fin de semana en la playa.

62. **Repasan:** Review
63. **Importante:** Important
64. **Bebidas:** Drinks
65. **Volver:** To return

66. **Olvidamos:** We forget

—Es mejor primero llegar a la carnicería, ya que falta poco para que la cierren —dice Pedro.

—Sí, lleguemos a la carnicería y cuando terminemos de comprar la carne necesaria, vamos al supermercado que su **hora** de cierre es más tarde —dice Carlos.

Al llegar a la carnicería, Pedro saluda al **carnicero** y **dueño** del **local** y le pide si podría ayudar a él y a sus amigos a escoger la carne de mejor calidad para el asado de la primera noche del viaje.

El carnicero se coloca detrás del **mostrador** y escoge diferentes cortes de carnes para que ellos mismos escojan lo que les parezca mejor y dice:

67. **Hora:** Hour
68. **Carnicero:** Butcher
69. **Dueño:** Owner
70. **Local:** Local
71. **Mostrador:** Counter

—Todo es carne de primera calidad, tienen **carne de res** y **costillas** que pueden combinar con unas muy jugosas **chuletas de cerdo** y muchas **alitas de pollo**.

72. **Carne de res:** Beef
73. **Costillas:** Ribs
74. **Chuletas de cerdo:** Pork chops
75. **Alitas de pollo:** Chicken wings

—Sabía que venir a esta carnicería sería la mejor elección; todo se ve de muy buena calidad —dice Pedro.

A lo que responden Michael y Carlos:

—Tienes razón, Pedro, todo se ve muy bueno y la atención es lo mejor —dice Michael.

—Pues sí, de tantas cosas buenas que nos muestra es mejor aprovechar y llevarse todo —dice Carlos con cara de **extasiado**.

A lo que el carnicero responde:

—Con esta carne, las chuletas de cerdo y las alitas de pollo les aseguro que harán una muy buena parrilla. ¿Cuánto quieren de cada uno?

—Creo que llevaremos dos **kilos** de cada tipo de carne, y así estamos seguros que no va faltar —responde Michael.

—Michael, recuerda que apenas será el primer día del viaje a la playa, solo con esa cena engordaremos unos cuantos kilos, luego no vamos a poder **exhibir** nuestros **musculosos** cuerpos —dice Pedro con **carcajadas**.

76. **Extasiado:** Ecstatic
77. **Kilos:** Kilograms
78. **Exhibir:** Exhibit
79. **Musculosos:** Muscular
80. **Carcajadas:** Laughter

—No importa, Pedro, después de ese gran caso que ganamos, nos lo merecemos. Después llegamos directo al gimnasio —dice Carlos entre risas.

—¡Listo!, voy a empacar todo en diferentes bandejas para que así sea fácil de transportar para el viaje de carretera —dice el carnicero.

Luego de que el carnicero les empacara los diferentes tipos de carne, Michael, Carlos y Pedro se disponen a pagar el total de la cuenta y le dejan una generosa propina por la grandiosa atención que reciben en la carnicería.

Regresan al carro y retoman la ruta hacia el supermercado, donde van a comprar las bebidas que todos habían olvidado de la lista.

Al llegar al supermercado, los recibe de nuevo la linda vendedora, María.

—Esperaba verlos pronto, pero no pensaba que sería tan pronto —dice María riéndose.

—Es que se nos ha olvidado algo muy importante, ¡las bebidas! —dice Michael.

—Nos acordamos cuando íbamos de salida de este supermercado, sino íbamos a pasar un fin de semana muy **sedientos** —dice Pedro.

—No se preocupen, en el pasillo número ocho pueden resolver ese problema, y así estarán bien **hidratados** durante su fin de semana —responde María sonriendo.

Los tres amigos se dirigen al pasillo número ocho y ven un estante de un par de metros con una gran variedad de bebidas.

Se disponen a escoger las **favoritas** de cada uno, sin olvidar que tienen que llevarse gran cantidad de **agua embotellada** para así aguantar el intenso calor en la playa.

81. **Sedientos:** Thirsty
82. **Hidratados:** Hydrated
83. **Favoritas:** Favorite
84. **Agua embotellada:** Bottled wáter

Al finalizar la elección de las bebidas, pagan por segunda vez en el supermercado y dice Michael:

—Esta vez sí tenemos todo lo de nuestra lista, ya estamos listos para el viaje. Solo falta que llegue el día del viaje.

—¡Y a celebrar! —dicen Carlos y Pedro al unísono y emocionados.

UN VIAJE AL SUPERMERCADO
PREGUNTAS

1. ¿Dónde compran Michael, Carlos y Pedro la comida necesaria para el viaje?

    a. En la playa

    b. En el supermercado

    c. En la casa

2. ¿Qué deciden que deben comprar primero?

    a. La carne para el asado

    b. Las verduras

    c. Las bebidas

3. ¿Qué les hace falta a Michael, Carlos y Pedro para preparar el Ceviche?

    a. Mariscos

    b. Chuletas de cerdo

    c. Alitas de pollo

4. ¿A dónde se dirigen luego de salir del supermercado?

    a. A la casa de Pedro

    b. A la carnicería

    c. A la playa

5. ¿Qué se les olvida colocar en la lista?

    a. La carne

    b. La lechuga

    c. Las bebidas

UN VIAJE AL SUPERMERCADO
SOLUCIONES

1. B

2. B

3. A

4. B

5. C

UN VIAJE AL SUPERMERCADO
VOCABULARIO

1. **Tarde:** Afternoon
2. **Hombre:** Man
3. **Corto viaje:** Short trip
4. **Abogados:** Lawyers
5. **Importante:** Important
6. **Premio:** Reward
7. **Playa:** Beach
8. **Anticipación:** Anticipation
9. **Ruta de carretera:** Road route
10. **Alquilar:** To rent
11. **Parrillera**: Barbecue
12. **Alimentos:** Food
13. **Diariamente:** Daily
14. **Asado:** Roast/Barbecue
15. **Mariscos:** Seafood
16. **Paseo:** Ride
17. **Supermercado:** Supermarket
18. **Compra:** Purchase
19. **Referente:** Concerning
20. **Verduras:** Vegetables
21. **Comida fresca:** Fresh food
22. **Trabajadora:** Worker
23. **Buscan:** Search
24. **Ensalada:** Salad
25. **Lechugas:** Lettuce
26. **Legumbres:** Legumes
27. **Elección:** Election
28. **Escoger:** To choose
29. **Tienda:** Store
30. **Inexperiencia:** Inexperience
31. **Detallada:** Detailed
32. **Mostrador:** Counter
33. **Necesitan:** They need (verb: necesitar)
34. **Ingredientes:** Ingredients
35. **Preparar:** To prepare
36. **Cebolla:** Onion
37. **Pimentón:** Paprika
38. **Productos del mar:** Products of the sea
39. **Refrigeradores:** Refrigerators
40. **Congelados:** Frozen
41. **Asombro:** Amazement
42. **Variedad:** Variety
43. **Gramos:** Grams

44. **Camarones:** Shrimp
45. **Calamares:** Squids
46. **Receta:** Recipe
47. **Enormes:** Huge
48. **Pasillos:** Corridors
49. **Lista:** List
50. **Sección:** Section
51. **Carnes:** Meats
52. **Parrilla:** Grill
53. **Calidad:** Quality
54. **Carnicería:** Butcher shop
55. **Caja registradora:** Cash register
56. **Pagar:** To pay
57. **Atención:** Attention
58. **Pronto:** Soon
59. **Carro:** Car
60. **Rápido:** Fast
61. **Cierre:** Closing
62. **Repasan:** Review
63. **Importante:** Important
64. **Bebidas:** Drinks
65. **Volver:** To return
66. **Olvidamos:** We forget/We forgot
67. **Hora:** Hour
68. **Carnicero:** Butcher
69. **Dueño:** Owner
70. **Local:** Local
71. **Mostrador:** Counter
72. **Carne de res:** Beef
73. **Costillas:** Ribs
74. **Chuletas de cerdo:** Pork chops
75. **Alitas de pollo:** Chicken wings
76. **Extasiado:** Captivated
77. **Kilos:** Kilograms
78. **Exhibir:** Exhibit
79. **Musculosos:** Muscular
80. **Carcajadas:** Laughter
81. **Sedientos:** Thirsty
82. **Hidratados:** Hydrated
83. **Favoritas:** Favorite
84. **Agua embotellada:** Bottled water

UN DISEÑO DE MUSEO
RESUMEN

Sofía, una joven de dieciocho años de edad, se muda a Manhattan, Nueva york persiguiendo el sueño de ser una famosa diseñadora de modas. La arquitectura citadina es una de las razones de su mudanza, piensa que la ayudaría a inspirarse para realizar diferentes bocetos de vestidos. Por lo cual junto a sus dos amigas Lauren y Mary Ann visitan el majestuoso Museo Metropolitano de Nueva York para buscar inspiración necesaria para sus trabajos finales en la escuela.

Sofía, an 18-year-old girl, moves to Manhattan, New York pursuing the dream of being a famous fashion designer. The city architecture is one of the reasons for her move; she thinks that it would help her to inspire herself to make different sketches of dresses. Which is why, together with her two friends Lauren and Mary Ann, they visit the majestic Metropolitan Museum of New York to find inspiration needed for their final works in school.

UN DISEÑO DE MUSEO

Sofía es una chica de dieciocho años que **reside** en Manhattan, Nueva York. Originaria de Atlanta, se **muda** de esa ciudad con el sueño de convertirse en una gran **diseñadora de modas**.

Estudia diseño de modas en la escuela de **artes** local. Va a la escuela junto con sus dos mejores amigas Lauren y Mary Ann, ambas de veinte años.

Lauren estudia **música** y Mary Ann toma clases de danza **contemporánea**.

A diferencia de Sofía, Lauren y Mary Ann nacieron en Manhattan, Nueva York, y desde pequeñas conocen cada **rincón** de la ciudad.

1. **Reside**: Resides
2. **Se muda:** Moves out
3. **Diseñadora de modas**: Fashion designer
4. **Artes**: Arts
5. **Música**: Music
6. **Contemporánea:** Contemporary
7. **Rincón**: Corner

Una de las razones del cambio de ciudad de Sofía, es la gran y variada **arquitectura** de la ciudad de Nueva York.

Sofía piensa que sus altos **edificios** y **construcciones** de **época**, pueden servirle como **inspiración** para muchos de sus diseños.

Diariamente Sofía camina por las calles de Manhattan, visualizando todos aquellos pequeños detalles de la arquitectura **citadina**.

8. **Arquitectura**: Architecture
9. **Edificios**: Buildings
10. **Construcciones**: Constructions
11. **Época:** Time
12. **Inspiración**: Inspiration
13. **Citadina:** Urban

Durante su caminata diaria, Sofía siempre se detiene en el **imponente** edificio del **Museo** Metropolitano de Arte de Nueva York.

Le llama la atención los numerosos **escalones** que conforman la **escalera** de la **fachada**, se imagina que pueden ser los **pliegues** de una gran falda.

Cada día, Sofía ha intentado entrar al museo, pero la larga **fila** que tiene que hacer para poder entrar la **desanima** un poco.

Un día, en la escuela de artes Sofía les plantea a sus amigas Lauren y Mary Ann que en su día libre lleguen temprano al Museo Metropolitano de Arte de Nueva York para así poder entrar y pasar el día viendo las **obras de arte** que allí exhiben.

Lauren y Mary Ann, poco convencidas de la idea de Sofía, ya que saben cómo son las largas filas que deben hacer para entrar, deciden investigar en internet la compra de una entrada con **privilegios**.

14. **Imponente**: Imposing
15. **Museo**: Museum
16. **Escalones:** Steps
17. **Escalera**: Stairs
18. **Desanima:** Discourage
19. **Fachada:** Facade
20. **Pliegues:** Pleats
21. **Fila**: Line
22. **Obras de arte**: Artworks
23. **Privilegios:** Privileges

Emocionadas por la compra de las entradas, Lauren y Mary Ann le dicen a Sofía:

—Te tenemos una gran sorpresa —dice Lauren.

—Después de esto, nos vas a querer **muchísimo** más —dice Mary Ann, riéndose.

—A ver, ¿Qué sorpresa me tienen?, por sus caras de emoción, no creo que sea algo **referente** al museo —responde Sofía desilusionada.

—Pues te equivocas, tenemos tres **entradas** al Museo Metropolitano de Arte, y lo mejor de todo es que... ¡No haremos la larga fila! —dice Lauren con tono de emoción.

—Ahora vamos a alistarnos para pasar un gran día en el museo —dice Mary Ann.

—Voy a preparar mi bolso, tengo que guardar la **cámara** y mi libreta de **dibujos**, para así no perder ni un segundo de inspiración —responde Sofía entusiasmada.

Llegado el día, Sofía, Lauren y Mary Ann se disponen a tomar un taxi para llegar a tiempo a las puertas de tan majestuosa **infraestructura**, suben corriendo los múltiples escalones y entregan sus entradas al **portero**.

24. **Muchísimo**: Very much
25. **Referente:** Related
26. **Entradas**: Tickets
27. **Cámara:** Camera
28. **Dibujos:** Drawings
29. **Infraestructura:** Infrastructure
30. **Portero:** Doorkeeper

—Buenos días, señoritas —dice el portero muy amablemente.

—Buenos días, señor —responden las tres chicas a una sola voz.

—¿Primera vez en el museo? —Pregunta el portero de manera curiosa.

A lo que Sofía responde:

—Para mí es la primera vez, siempre lo he querido **conocer** y por eso me siento muy entusiasmada.

—Lo pude notar en tu cara, van a pasar un **interesante** día en las instalaciones del museo, no puedes perderte ningún detalle —acota el portero.

—No lo voy a hacer, vine preparada con mi cámara y mi libreta de dibujos para así no pasar nada por alto —dice Sofía.

El portero recibe los tickets de Sofía, Lauren y Mary Ann y les da la **bienvenida** al museo.

Una vez pasada la puerta principal, Sofía no puede ocultar lo emocionada que está, ya que por fin ha logrado entrar a uno de los lugares más esperados que se ha **propuesto** conocer de la ciudad.

31. **Conocer**: To know
32. **Interesante**: Interesting
33. **Bienvenida**: Welcome
34. **Propuesto**: Proposed

Sofía, Lauren y Mary Ann están impactadas por todo lo que ven, cada sala tiene un tipo de obra de arte distinta, desde tesoros de la **antigüedad** clásica, a **pinturas** y **esculturas** de casi todos los **maestros** de Europa y una gran colección de obras estadounidenses.

Lauren y Mary Ann le comentan a Sofía:

—Esto es impresionante, recuerdo la última vez que estuve aquí y nada es igual —dice Lauren.

—Me pasa lo mismo, de tantas cosas que hay para **apreciar**, parece que esta fuera la primera vez para mí también. Sé que te va a encantar Sofía —dice Mary Ann.

—No quiero perderme de ningún **detalle**, esto me va a ayudar mucho para la inspiración de mis nuevos diseños —dice Sofía.

35. **Antigüedad**: Antiquity
36. **Pinturas**: Paintings
37. **Esculturas**: Sculptures
38. **Maestros**: Teachers
39. **Apreciar:** To appreciate
40. **Detalle:** Detail

—Después de salir de aquí, Mary Ann y yo tendremos muchos **vestidos** nuevos —dice Lauren con **picardía**.

Las tres chicas se acercan al salón de la recepción y toman los **folletos** donde indican los diferentes **departamentos** del Museo Metropolitano de Arte, y entonces Sofía dice:

—Creo que quiero comenzar a ver la **exhibición** expuesta en el **edificio principal**. Aquí dice que hay más de seis mil **objetos expuestos**, de ahí puedo sacar mi primer **boceto**.

41. **Vestidos**: Dresses
42. **Picardía:** Mischief
43. **Folletos**: Brochures
44. **Departamentos**: Departments
45. **Exhibición**: Display/Exhibition
46. **Edificio principal:** Main building
47. **Objetos:** Objects
48. **Expuestos** Exposed
49. **Boceto:** Sketch

—**Caminemos** hasta allá y veamos qué tiene el edificio principal —le dice Mary Ann a Sofía y Lauren.

Al llegar al edificio principal, se dan cuenta de los numerosos objetos ahí exhibidos, desde **tapices** hasta **estatuas** muy grandes.

Sofía se sienta en una **banca** y **busca** en su **bolso** su **libreta** y **lápiz**, mira **con detenimiento** uno de los tapices **exhibidos** y comienza a realizar **garabatos** en la libreta.

50. **Caminemos:** Let's walk (verb:caminar)
51. **Tapices**: Hangings
52. **Estatuas**: Statues
53. **Banca**: Bench
54. **Busca**: Searches
55. **Bolso**: Handbag
56. **Libreta**: Notebook
57. **Lápiz:** Pencil
58. **Con detenimiento:** Thoroughly
59. **Exhibidos**: Exhibited
60. **Garabatos**: Scribbles

—¡Ya tengo mi primer diseño! —exclama Sofía.

—¿Para quién será?, ¿para mí o para Mary Ann? —pregunta Lauren de manera **graciosa**.

—Chicas, esto es para mi **escuela** de **arte**. Cuando sea **famosa** ustedes usarán mis diseños gratis —dice Sofía a sus dos amigas.

—Bueno, Sofía, esperemos que de esta visita al museo salgan muchos bocetos de vestidos **hermosos** que te harán famosa muy rápido —dice Mary Ann.

Al finalizar de ver la exhibición expuesta en el edificio principal, Sofía, Lauren y Mary Ann acuerdan visitar ahora las **galerías** secundarias que dice el folleto.

Según el folleto, ahí se exponen piezas más pequeñas en **metales** preciosos y **marfil**.

61. **Graciosa:** Funny
62. **Escuela**: School
63. **Arte:** Art
64. **Famosa**: Famous
65. **Hermosos**: Beautiful
66. **Galerías**: Galleries
67. **Metales**: Metals
68. **Marfil:** Ivory

Por lo que Sofía dice:

—De las galerías secundarias puedo inspirarme para diseñar vestidos más modernos, llenos de metales y piedras preciosas ideales para una **gala** en la noche.

—Estoy segura que esos serán los mejores diseños de tu **clase,** Sofía, con esta fuente de inspiración tan espectacular que tienes en el museo —dice Lauren.

—Yo también estoy segura de eso, vas a obtener una muy buena **calificación** —responde Mary Ann con entusiasmo.

Sofía, Lauren y Mary Ann llegan a una de las galerías secundarias y quedan impresionadas por una **pequeña** obra de arte de marfil con miles de detalles.

69. **Gala**: Gala
70. **Clase**: Class
71. **Calificación:** Grade

72. **Pequeña**: Little

Mary Ann y Sofía se quedan comentando lo impresionante de esa obra en miniatura, preguntándose cómo puede inspirarse Sofía en su próximo diseño.

Lauren ve a lo lejos de la galería secundaria una pequeña **cafetería** y les comenta Lauren a sus dos amigas:

—Es hora de tomar un pequeño **descanso**. Podemos ir a la pequeña cafetería y les invito un café.

—Buena idea, ya tengo hambre y ahorita no encuentro inspiración —dice Sofía algo desilusionada.

—Entonces un descanso te viene bien —dice Mary Ann animando a Sofía.

Llegan a la cafetería, cada una ordena un **aperitivo** y un café y conversan sobre cómo ha sido la experiencia de visitar el Museo Metropolitano de Arte de Nueva York.

Luego de haber terminado su descanso, ven el folleto y les llama la atención el departamento en donde se expone la **colección** de **instrumentos musicales**, una de las exhibiciones más importantes del mundo, ya que es casi única entre los museos.

73. **Cafetería:** Cafeteria
74. **Descanso:** Break
75. **Aperitivo**: Appetizer
76. **Colección**: Collection
77. **Instrumentos musicales:** Musical instruments

En el salón hay miles de instrumentos de toda clase y época que han sido tocados por famosos músicos de la historia.

Sofía ve en la mitad del salón un **imponente** piano en el cual una reseña dice que es el **piano** más antiguo del mundo, un modelo del año 1720.

Es por ese piano que Sofía se inspira para crear el boceto de un hermoso vestido negro con una **gran cola**, parecido a la parte posterior de aquel piano que ve en el museo, con detalles en color blanco que se **asemejan** a las **teclas**, y poder así presentarlo en la escuela de arte como su trabajo final.

78. **Imponente**: Imposing
79. **Piano**: Piano
80. **Gran cola:** Great tail
81. **Asemejan**: Resemble
82. **Teclas:** Keys (of a piano)

Llega el final del recorrido y Sofía, Lauren y Mary Ann satisfechas por la visita al museo comentan entre ellas:

—**No me arrepiento** en haber venido, me encanta este lugar y lo visitaré muchas veces más —comenta Lauren.

—La verdad es que sí, voy a estar **revisando** en internet cada vez que pueda para que compremos las mismas entradas y no tengamos que hacer largas filas —dice Mary Ann.

—Quiero venir todos los días y así inspirarme en cada obra de arte del museo para mis bocetos. Con una sola visita no se puede ver toda la exhibición —dice Sofía.

—Y cada vez que vengas, te vamos a **acompañar**, ten eso por seguro —le dice Lauren a su amiga Sofía.

Varios días después, Sofía entrega su trabajo final en la escuela de artes y obtiene la **mejor** calificación de la clase.

83. **No me arrepiento**: I don't regret

84. **Revisando**: Checking

85. **Acompañar:** Accompany

86. **Mejor**: Best

UN DISEÑO DE MUSEO
PREGUNTAS

1. ¿Cuál es el sueño de Sofía?

    a. Ser músico

    b. Ser diseñadora de modas

    c. Ser bailarina de danza contemporánea

2. ¿Cómo compran las entradas del museo?

    a. Por internet

    b. En una subasta

    c. Haciendo la cola en el museo

3. ¿Quién va por primera vez al museo?

    a. Sofía

    b. Lauren

    c. Mary Ann

4. ¿Por qué Sofía queda impresionada en la galería secundaria?

    a. Por el piano

    b. Por los metales preciosos

    c. Por la obra de arte de marfil

5. ¿En qué se inspiró para su diseño final?

    a. Tapiz

    b. Piano

    c. Escultura de marfil

UN DISEÑO DE MUSEO
SOLUCIONES

1. B

2. A

3. A

4. C

5. B

UN DISEÑO DE MUSEO
VOCABULARIO

1. **Reside**: Resides
2. **Muda:** Moves out
3. **Diseñadora de modas**: Fashion designer
4. **Artes**: Arts
5. **Música**: Music
6. **Contemporánea:** Contemporary
7. **Rincón**: Corner
8. **Arquitectura**: Architecture
9. **Edificios**: Buildings
10. **Construcciones**: Constructions
11. **Época:** Time
12. **Inspiración**: Inspiration
13. **Citadina:** Urban
14. **Imponente**: Imposing
15. **Museo**: Museum
16. **Escalones:** Steps
17. **Escalera**: Stairs
18. **Desanima:** Discourage
19. **Fachada:** Facade
20. **Pliegues:** Pleats
21. **Fila**: Line
22. **Obras de arte**: Artworks
23. **Privilegios:** Privileges
24. **Muchísimo**: Very much
25. **Referente:** Related
26. **Entradas**: Tickets
27. **Cámara:** Camera
28. **Dibujos:** Drawings
29. **Infraestructura:** Infrastructure
30. **Portero:** Doorkeeper
31. **Conocer:** To Know
32. **Interesante**: Interesting
33. **Bienvenida**: Welcome
34. **Propuesto**: Proposed
35. **Antigüedad**: Antiquity
36. **Pinturas**: Paintings
37. **Esculturas**: Sculptures
38. **Maestros**: Teachers
39. **Apreciar:** To appreciate
40. **Detalle**: Detail
41. **Vestidos**: Dresses
42. **Picardía**: Mischief
43. **Folletos**: Brochures

44. **Departamentos**: Departments
45. **Exhibición**: Display/Exhibition
46. **Edificio principal:** Main building
47. **Objetos:** Objects
48. **Expuestos:** Exposed
49. **Boceto:** Sketch
50. **Caminemos:** Let's walk (Verb:Caminar)
51. **Tapices**: Hangings
52. **Estatuas**: Statues
53. **Banca**: Bench
54. **Busca**: Searches
55. **Bolso**: Handbag
56. **Libreta**: Notebook
57. **Lápiz:** Pencil
58. **Con detenimiento:** Thoroughly
59. **Exhibidos**: Exhibited
60. **Garabatos**: Scribbles
61. **Graciosa:** Funny
62. **Escuela**: School
63. **Arte:** Art
64. **Famosa**: Famous
65. **Hermosos**: Beautiful
66. **Galerías**: Galleries
67. **Metales**: Metals
68. **Marfil:** Ivory
69. **Gala**: Gala
70. **Clase**: Class
71. **Calificación:** Grade
72. **Pequeña**: Little
73. **Cafetería:** Cafeteria
74. **Descanso:** Break
75. **Aperitivo**: Appetizer
76. **Colección**: Collection
77. **Instrumentos musicales:** Musical instruments
78. **Imponente**: Imposing
79. **Piano**: Piano
80. **Gran cola:** Great tail
81. **Asemejan**: Resemble
82. **Teclas:** Keys (of a piano)
83. **No me arrepiento:** I don't regret
84. **Revisando**: Checking
85. **Acompañar:** Accompany
86. **Mejor**: Best

MARAVILLOSAMENTE NATURAL
RESUMEN

Carla y Ricardo son una pareja de novios que aman la naturaleza. Ella ocasionalmente trabaja con la reforestación de algunas zonas necesitadas y él es fotógrafo de exteriores. En tres meses se van a casar y planifican todos los detalles de su luna de miel. Como a ambos les gusta viajar, harán un viaje por carretera desde Argentina hasta Venezuela, donde está el destino final de su luna de miel, La Gran Sabana venezolana. También van a visitar la cascada más alta del mundo, el Salto Ángel, para así tomar muchas hermosas fotografías de cada uno de los paisajes.

Carla and Ricardo are a couple who love nature. She occasionally works with the reforestation of some areas in need and he is an outdoor photographer. In three months they will get married and plan all the details of their honeymoon. As both of them like to travel, they will make a road trip from Argentina to Venezuela, where the final destination of their honeymoon is located, Venezuela's Gran Sabana. They will also visit the highest waterfall in the world, the Salto Angel, to take many beautiful photographs of each of the landscapes.

MARAVILLOSAMENTE NATURAL

Carla y Ricardo son una **pareja** de **novios**. Tienen veintiséis y veintinueve años **respectivamente**, viven en Buenos Aires, Argentina y piensan **casarse** en tres meses.

Carla es amante de la **naturaleza**, siempre participa como **voluntaria** para la **reforestación** de lugares que lo necesitan.

1. **Pareja:** Couple
2. **Novios:** Boyfriend and girlfriend
3. **Respectivamente:** Respectively
4. **Casarse:** To get married
5. **Naturaleza:** Nature
6. **Voluntaria:** Volunteer
7. **Reforestación:** Reforestation

Ricardo es un **fotógrafo** especialista en **fotografía de exterior**. Ha viajado alrededor del mundo buscando **paisajes** hermosos para tomar la foto perfecta.

Carla y Ricardo **se conocieron** en un viaje a un **bosque**, congeniaron de inmediato y después de ese viaje se volvieron **inseparables**.

Sus conversaciones siempre son del mismo tema, el próximo **destino** que a los dos les gustaría visitar.

8. **Fotógrafo:** Photographer
9. **Fotografía de exterior:** Exterior photography
10. **Paisajes:** Landscapes
11. **Se conocieron:** They met each other (verb: conocer)
12. **Bosque:** Forest
13. **Inseparables:** Inseparable
14. **Destino:** Destination

Siempre discuten por ir a la **playa**, a la **montaña** o a una **zona desértica**, pero desde el momento de su compromiso, estuvieron de acuerdo que su **luna de miel** sería en la Gran Sabana, Venezuela.

Desde hace meses Carla y Ricardo se han **propuesto** investigar cada detalle del recorrido, **clima**, **flora**, **fauna** y todo lo referente a ese viaje tan esperado.

15. **Playa:** Beach
16. **Montaña:** Mountain
17. **Zona desértica:** Desert area
18. **Luna de miel:** Honeymoon
19. **Propuesto:** Proposed
20. **Clima:** Weather
21. **Flora:** Flora
22. **Fauna:** Fauna

Un día Carla, se sienta en frente de su **computadora personal** y se dispone a buscar en un buscador de internet el **recorrido** por **carretera** desde Buenos Aires, Argentina hasta Bolívar, Venezuela, el **estado** donde está ubicada la maravilla natural llamada La Gran Sabana, en la selva Amazónica.

Emocionada por su hallazgo, Carla llama a su futuro esposo al celular y dice:

—Mi amor, he encontrado el recorrido por carretera perfecto para llegar a nuestro destino de luna de miel.

23. **Computadora personal:** Personal computer
24. **Recorrido:** Route
25. **Carretera:** Highway
26. **Estado:** State

—¿Por carretera? —pregunta Ricardo exaltado.

A lo que Carla responde:

—Sí, mi amor, estaba pensando que irnos de luna de miel por **vía terrestre** va a ser una experiencia inolvidable.

—Tienes razón, viajar hasta La Gran Sabana por carretera es muy buena idea —le responde Ricardo a Carla con voz llena de **emoción**.

—Una de las razones por la cual he pensado en la idea de irnos por vía terrestre es que puedes bajarte del carro en cada paisaje que te guste y así tomar muy buenas **fotografías** —dice Carla.

Ricardo no puede esperar a llegar a **casa** de Carla para ver y **estudiar** esa **ruta** de la que tanto hablaba Carla y le dice:

27. **Vía terrestre:** Land route
28. **Emoción:** Emotion
29. **Fotografías:** Photographs
30. **Casa:** House
31. **Estudiar:** Study
32. **Ruta:** Route

—Termino con estas **diligencias** que estoy haciendo y corro a tu casa a verlo con mis **propios** ojos.

Carla responde con unas **carcajadas** y termina la **llamada** diciendo:

33. **Diligencias:** Errands
34. **Propios:** Own
35. **Carcajadas:** Laughter
36. **Llamada:** Call

—Aquí te espero, mi amor.

Al finalizar con las diligencias que realizaba, Ricardo se sube muy rápido a su **carro** y toma la **vía** más rápida para llegar a casa de Carla.

Cuando ambos están en frente de la computadora personal, en la **página** de internet referente a las rutas desde Buenos Aires a La Gran Sabana, deciden si irse por la ruta de Brasil o la ruta por Colombia. Y entonces conversan:

—Creo que es **mejor** la ruta por Brasil, es más **económica** y son solo nueve días. Además **atravesaremos** el Amazonas que es **bellísimo** y puedes tomar fotos increíbles —dice Carla.

37. **Carro:** Car
38. **Vía:** Route
39. **Página:** Page
40. **Mejor:** Better
41. **Económica:** Economical
42. **Atravesaremos:** We will cross
43. **Bellísimo:** Beautiful

—¿Y la ruta por Colombia? —pregunta Ricardo.

—Es más **larga**, son más de nueve días y después no disfrutaremos todas las **actividades** que hay por **hacer** en La Gran Sabana —le responde Carla con la intención de **planificar** a la perfección su luna de miel.

44. **Larga:** Long
45. **Actividades:** Activities
46. **Hacer:** To do
47. **Planificar:** To plan

—Entonces... ¡Está **decidido**!, Brasil es la ruta para llegar a La Gran Sabana, me siento muy **emocionado** —le dice Ricardo a su novia.

Pasan los días y el día de la **boda** llega. **Nervioso** y **entusiasmado** por el gran momento, Ricardo hace una confesión por medio de un **mensaje de texto** que le envía a su futura esposa. Minutos antes de encontrarse en el **altar** él dice:

48. **Decidido:** Decided
49. **Emocionado:** Excited
50. **Boda:** Wedding
51. **Nervioso:** Nervous
52. **Entusiasmado:** Excited
53. **Mensaje de texto:** Text message
54. **Altar:** Altar

«Me siento muy emocionado porque hoy te **conviertas** en mi **amada** esposa, pero tengo algo que decirte... Estoy mucho más emocionado porque nuestros primeros días como **esposos** los pasaremos en LA GRAN SABANA».

A Carla se le dibuja una gran **sonrisa** en la cara y le **responde** por la misma vía:

«Lo mismo me pasa, ya quiero llegar allá, nos vemos en el altar, con amor, tu **casi** esposa».

La boda ha terminado, y los ahora esposos **emprenden** su viaje de carretera desde Buenos Aires, Argentina hasta Bolívar, Venezuela, para así llegar a su tan esperado destino, la **maravillosa** Gran Sabana.

55. **Conviertas:** Become
56. **Amada:** Loved

57. **Esposos:** Husband and wife

58. **Sonrisa:** Smile

59. **Responde:** Answers

60. **Casi:** Almost

61. **Emprenden:** Undertake

62. **Maravillosa:** Wonderful

Ya han pasado varios días en la ruta, tomando fotos increíbles de toda la **zona selvática** del Amazonas y disfrutando de sus primeros días de casados en la vía. Hasta que por fin Carla y Ricardo llegan a la **frontera** que une a Brasil con Venezuela.

Y preguntan a un señor de la zona:

—Buenos días, señor. ¿Cuánto nos falta para llegar al estado de Bolívar? —pregunta Ricardo ansioso por llegar a su destino.

A lo que responde el señor:

—No les falta nada, ya están en Bolívar. ¿Hacia dónde se **dirigen**?

—A La Gran Sabana —responde Carla.

—Pues, ya les falta muy poco para llegar, **disfruten** cada momento de la maravilla natural que nos regaló el **universo** —dice el Señor.

—Muchas gracias, señor, muy **amable** —responden ambos y siguen su **rumbo**.

63. **Zona selvática:** Jungle area

64. **Frontera:** Border

65. **Dirigen:** Head for

66. **Disfruten:** Enjoy

67. **Universo:** Universe

68. **Amable:** Kind

69. **Rumbo:** Course

Al entrar más en el estado Bolívar, empiezan a observar todo en su alrededor y ven que están rodeados de majestuosas formaciones parecidas a las montañas, llamadas tepuyes.

—Esto es **increíble**, tus fotos quedaran muy **hermosas** —le dice Carla a su esposo.

—Estoy muy impresionado, a cada lugar que mires, ves una **cascada**, un **río**, un **valle** o una **tupida selva** —dice Ricardo con voz llena de emoción.

—Empieza a tomar fotos, no podemos quedarnos sin tomarle una fotografía a cada milímetro de este hermoso paisaje —dice Carla **extasiada** por lo que sus ojos están mirando.

70. **Increíble:** Incredible
71. **Hermosas:** Beautiful
72. **Cascada:** Waterfall
73. **Río:** River
74. **Valle:** Valley
75. **Tupida:** Dense
76. **Selva:** Jungle
77. **Extasiada:** Ecstatic

—Sí, mi amor, le tomaré foto a cada milímetro de este paisaje. Creo que serán las mejores fotos de toda mi **carrera** —le comenta Ricardo a Carla.

—Yo también lo creo. Ahora llegaremos a una **posada** y mañana vamos a visitar el **Parque** Nacional Canaima —dice Carla.

—¿De verdad? ¿Mañana es el día que vamos a visitar el Parque Nacional Canaima? Entonces vamos a conocer la cascada más **alta** del **mundo**, ¡el Salto Ángel! —dice Ricardo muy excitado.

78. **Carrera:** Career
79. **Posada:** Inn
80. **Parque:** Park
81. **Alta:** High
82. **Mundo:** World

—Veo que **investigaste** sobre este lugar —dice Carla entre risas, ya que ve a su esposo muy emocionado por la visita del día siguiente.

—¿Cómo llegaremos hasta allá? —pregunta Ricardo en tono curioso.

—He comprado dos tickets de **avioneta** para **sobrevolar** por la selva amazónica y llegar hasta el Salto Ángel —responde Carla.

—Estoy muy ansioso porque el día de mañana llegue. Me iré a dormir **temprano** para que la noche se pase más rápido —dice Ricardo muy entusiasmado.

A lo que responde Carla:

—Nunca **imaginé** verte tan emocionado. Lo que decía aquel mensaje de texto el día de nuestra boda ahora puedo ver que es verdad —dice Carla impresionada por la reacción de su esposo a la visita del Salto Ángel.

83. **Investigaste:** investigated
84. **Avioneta:** Light aircraft
85. **Sobrevolar:** To overfly
86. **Temprano:** Early
87. **Imaginé:** Imagined

Pasa la noche, y llega el día de la gran visita, toman la avioneta y empiezan a sobrevolar la zona selvática del Amazona.

Impactados por lo que ven al llegar al lugar donde se encuentre la gran cascada del Salto Ángel, comentan entre ellos:

—Esto es verdaderamente **impresionante**. Parecemos unas pequeñas **hormigas** al lado de tan **majestuosa maravilla natural**. Tomaré unas fotografías aéreas para que se vea lo profundo de la caída del agua —dice Ricardo.

88. **Impactado:** Impacted
89. **Impresionante:** Impressive
90. **Hormigas:** Ants
91. **Majestuosa:** Majestic
92. **Maravilla natural:** Natural wonder

—Tómalas, así cuando bajemos de la avioneta, tendrás dos **tomas** distintas del Salto Ángel —responde Carla.

Al bajar de la avioneta, Carla y Ricardo toman una pequeña **embarcación**, manejada por un **indígena** de la zona, que los lleva a la parte final de la cascada, cruzando así la selva por **vía acuática**.

Al llegar a la parte final de la cascada, Carla y Ricardo se detienen y observan detenidamente el hermoso paisaje, escuchando el cantar de las **aves** de la zona y sintiendo en su cuerpo las **gotas** que caen desde lo más alto de la cascada.

93. **Tomas:** Shots (photography)
94. **Embarcación:** Boat
95. **Indígena:** Indigenous
96. **Vía acuática:** Waterway
97. **Aves:** Birds
98. **Gotas:** Drops

Y comentan:

—Todavía no creo lo que veo, esto parece mentira, es simplemente ¡perfecto! —comenta Carla.

—Por fin estoy viendo con mis propios ojos lo que vi en varias películas. Empezaré a tomar fotografías de esta belleza —dice Ricardo con cara de impresión.

—¡Yo me siento en una **película**! —exclama Carla—. Ver la corriente de agua caer por ese **tepuy** parece un efecto especial de las mejores **producciones** del cine.

99. **Película:** Movie
100. **Tepuy:** Regional name for mesa or table top mountain
101. **Producciones:** Productions

Ricardo comienza a tomar miles de fotos a cada centímetro de la cascada y de los tepuyes que la rodean, así como también del río en donde desemboca.

Sin darse cuenta habían pasado horas observando el paisaje y al caer la tarde ven el sol ocultándose por detrás de la parte más alta del Salto Ángel y dicen:

—Lo que veo parece una pintura del pintor más famoso del mundo, no tiene ningún error, no hace falta **editar** las fotos que he tomado hoy —dice Ricardo.

—¿Tomaste la mejor fotografía de toda tu carrera? —le pregunta Carla a su esposo.

—¡Sí! —responde **firmemente**—. Y esta ha sido la mejor luna de miel de mi vida.

A lo que responde Carla entre risas:

—Y espero que haya sido y siempre sea la única que tengas.

Ambos, entre carcajadas, concluyen que visitar La Gran Sabana es una experiencia inolvidable y que va a quedar **grabada** en su mente y en sus hermosas fotografías.

102. **Editar:** Edit
103. **Firmemente:** Firmly
104. **Grabada:** Recorded

MARAVILLOSAMENTE NATURAL
PREGUNTAS

1. ¿Dónde se conocieron Carla y Ricardo?

    a. En un viaje a la sabana

    b. En un viaje al bosque

    c. En un viaje a la cascada

2. ¿Qué ruta escogen para llegar a Venezuela?

    a. La ruta por Colombia

    b. La ruta por Ecuador

    c. La ruta por Brasil

3. ¿Cómo se llaman las formaciones parecidas a las montañas?

    a. Tepuyes

    b. Cascadas

    c. Ríos

4. ¿Por qué se siente ansioso Ricardo?

    a. Por conocer el Salto Ángel

    b. Porque se haga de noche

    c. Por viajar en avioneta

5. ¿Cómo llegan Carla y Ricardo a la parte final de la cascada?

    a. En avioneta

    b. En una embarcación

    c. En carro

MARAVILLOSAMENTE NATURAL
SOLUCIONES

1. B

2. C

3. A

4. A

5. B

MARAVILLOSAMENTE NATURAL
VOCABULARIO

1. **Pareja:** Couple
2. **Novios:** Boyfriend and girlfriend
3. **Respectivamente:** Respectively
4. **Casarse:** To get married
5. **Naturaleza:** Nature
6. **Voluntaria:** Volunteer
7. **Reforestación:** Reforestation
8. **Fotógrafo:** Photographer
9. **Fotografía de exterior:** Exterior photography
10. **Paisajes:** Landscapes
11. **Se conocieron:** They met each other(verb: conocer)
12. **Bosque:** Forest
13. **Inseparables:** Inseparable
14. **Destino:** Destination
15. **Playa:** Beach
16. **Montaña:** Mountain
17. **Zona desértica:** Desert area
18. **Luna de miel:** Honeymoon
19. **Propuesto:** Proposed
20. **Clima:** Weather
21. **Flora:** Flora
22. **Fauna:** Fauna
23. **Computadora personal:** Personal computer
24. **Recorrido:** Route
25. **Carretera:** Highway
26. **Estado:** State
27. **Vía terrestre:** Land route
28. **Emoción:** Emotion
29. **Fotografías:** Photographs
30. **Casa:** House
31. **Estudiar:** Study
32. **Ruta:** Route
33. **Diligencias:** Errands
34. **Propios:** Own
35. **Carcajadas:** Laughter
36. **Llamada:** Call
37. **Carro:** Car

38. **Vía:** Route
39. **Página:** Page
40. **Mejor:** Better
41. **Económica:** Economical
42. **Atravesaremos:** We will cross
43. **Bellísimo:** Beautiful
44. **Larga:** Long
45. **Actividades:** Activities
46. **Hacer:** To do
47. **Planificar:** To plan
48. **Decidido:** Decided
49. **Emocionado:** Excited
50. **Boda:** Wedding
51. **Nervioso:** Nervous
52. **Entusiasmado:** Excited
53. **Mensaje de texto:** Text message
54. **Altar:** Altar
55. **Conviertas:** become
56. **Amada:** Loved
57. **Esposos:** Husband and wife
58. **Sonrisa:** Smile
59. **Responde:** Answers
60. **Casi:** Almost
61. **Emprenden:** Undertake
62. **Maravillosa:** Wonderful
63. **Zona selvática:** Jungle area
64. **Frontera:** Border
65. **Dirigen:** Head for
66. **Disfruten:** Enjoy
67. **Universo:** Universe
68. **Amable:** Kind
69. **Rumbo:** Course
70. **Increíble:** Incredible
71. **Hermosas:** Beautiful
72. **Cascada:** Waterfall
73. **Río:** River
74. **Valle:** Valley
75. **Tupida:** Dense
76. **Selva:** Jungle
77. **Extasiada:** Ecstatic
78. **Carrera:** Career
79. **Posada:** Inn
80. **Parque:** Park
81. **Alta:** High
82. **Mundo:** World
83. **Investigaste:** investigated
84. **Avioneta:** Light aircraft
85. **Sobrevolar:** To overfly
86. **Temprano:** Early
87. **Imaginé:** Imagined

88. **Impactado:** Impacted

89. **Impresionante:** Impressive

90. **Hormigas:** Ants

91. **Majestuosa:** Majestic

92. **Maravilla natural:** Natural wonder

93. **Tomas:** Shots (photography)

94. **Embarcación:** Boat

95. **Indígena:** Indigenous

96. **Vía acuática:** Waterway

97. **Aves:** Birds

98. **Gotas:** Drops

99. **Película:** Movie

100. **Tepuy:** Regional name for mesa or table top mountain

101. **Producciones:** Productions

102. **Editar:** To edit

103. **Firmemente:** Firmly

104. **Grabada:** Recorded

EL AS BAJO LA MANGA
RESUMEN

Frank, un chico de veintiocho años, decide emprender su vida en un nuevo país y experimentar lo que es vivir solo. Un día recibe la noticia que sus dos amigos del colegio vendrán a visitarlo y así podrán disfrutar de los inmensos placeres culinarios que Maracaibo ofrece.

Frank, a 28-year-old boy, decides to start his life in a new country and experience what it is to live alone. One day he receives the news that his two friends from the school will come to visit him and thus, they will be able to enjoy the immense culinary pleasures that Maracaibo offers.

EL AS BAJO LA MANGA

Frank es un chico de veintiocho años, **graduado** de **periodista** en Perú, **actualmente viviendo** en la **ciudad** de Maracaibo, Venezuela. Se encuentra **experimentando** la vida de **soltero** viviendo en un **apartamento** tipo **estudio**.

1. **Graduado**: Graduate
2. **Periodista**: Journalist
3. **Actualmente**: Currently
4. **Viviendo:** Living
5. **Ciudad**: City
6. **Experimentando**: Experiencing
7. **Soltero**: Single
8. **Apartamento**: Apartment
9. **Estudio:** Studio

Toda la vida Frank se ha **caracterizado** por ser el **centro** de **atención**, **presidente** estudiantil de su **colegio** y presidente de la **sociedad** de **estudiantes** de su **universidad**.

10. **Caracterizado**: Characterized
11. **Centro**: Center
12. **Atención:** Attention
13. **Presidente**: President
14. **Colegio:** School
15. **Sociedad**: Society
16. **Estudiantes**: Students
17. **Universidad:** College

Se encuentra muy **emocionado** ya que sus dos **mejores** amigos del colegio vienen a visitarlo desde la ciudad de Lima, Perú. Pasarán dos **semanas** de **vacaciones** junto a su amigo Frank.

Ansioso por la **llegada** de sus dos amigos Ángel y Armando, Frank había **comprado** comida y bebidas para diez personas, **siendo** ellos tan solo tres personas.

Llega el día de la **visita**. Frank los espera en el **aeropuerto** con una **pancarta** de un metro por un metro aproximadamente, con un **mensaje chistoso** de cosas que se decían en el colegio, que solo ellos iban a entender.

18. **Emocionado**: Excited
19. **Mejores**: Best
20. **Semanas:** Weeks
21. **Vacaciones**: Vacation
22. **Ansioso**: Anxious
23. **Llegada**: Arrival

24. **Comprado**: Bought (verb: comprar)

25. **Siendo:** Being

26. **Visita:** Visit

27. **Aeropuerto:** Airport

28. **Pancarta**: Banner

29. **Mensaje**: Message

30. **Chistoso**: Funny

Frank Grita:

—¡Chicos, por aquí!

A lo **lejos** se ven Ángel y Armando **acercándose** a un paso **rápido**, ambos cargaban dos **maletas** grandes **como si fueran** a **quedarse** tres meses de visita en Venezuela.

—Frank, qué gusto **verte** —dicen Ángel y Armando.

Se **saludan** con un fuerte **abrazo** y Frank responde:

—**Tiempo** sin vernos, creo que la **última** vez fue hace dos años.

—Claro, la última vez fue cuando nos visitaste allá en Perú, en el **cumpleaños** de mi hermana Violeta, la pasamos muy bien ese día —dijo Ángel.

31. **Lejos**: Far

32. **Acercándose:** Approaching

33. **Rápido:** Quick

34. **Maletas**: Suitcases

35. **Como si fueran:** As if they were going to

36. **Quedarse:** To stay

37. **Verte**: To see you (verb: ver)

38. **Saludan**: Greet

39. **Abrazo**: Hug

40. **Tiempo**: Time

41. **Última:** Last
42. **Cumpleaños**: Birthday

Se sentaron a **conversar** en unos **sillones** que se veían a lo lejos y cuando menos se dieron cuenta, ya habían estado conversando una hora. En ese momento Armando dice:

—Frank, ¿será que podemos ir a comer algo?, me estoy **muriendo de hambre** y estoy seguro que Ángel también. Sabes que nosotros tres vivimos para **comer**.

—Claro que sí, vamos a comer unas hamburguesas que quedan en un **puesto de comida callejera** cerca de la casa, les aseguro que no se arrepentirán —dice Frank.

Durante todo el **trayecto** desde el **aeropuerto** hasta el puesto de comida, Ángel y Armando contaron no menos de diez sitios para comer que querían visitar antes de irse.

Llegan al puesto de comida. Frank le dice al **taxista** que también era un conocido personal de él, que los fuera a buscar cuando terminaran de comer.

43. **Conversar:** To converse
44. **Sillones**: Armchairs
45. **Muriendo de hambre**: Starving
46. **Comer:** To eat
47. **Puesto de comida callejera:** Street food stand
48. **Trayecto:** Journey
49. **Aeropuerto:** Airport
50. **Taxista**: Taxi driver

Luego de pasar diez minutos leyendo el menú e **indecisos** acerca de lo que quieren comer, porque todo sonaba muy **delicioso**, el **encargado** del lugar les dice:

—**Bienvenidos**, veo que están un poco indecisos, ¿los puedo ayudar a tomar la decisión de lo que quieren comer?

Ángel responde:

—Es que todo suena delicioso, pero estoy entre la **doble hamburguesa de queso fundido** y la hamburguesa con pollo **crujiente**.

51. **Indecisos:** Undecided
52. **Delicioso:** Delicious
53. **Encargado**: Manager
54. **Bienvenidos:** Welcome
55. **Doble hamburguesa de queso fundido:** Double cheese burger
56. **Crujiente:** Crunchy

El encargado responde entre risas:

—Dura **decisión**, pero le recomiendo la doble hamburguesa de queso fundido ya que es más grande que la hamburguesa con pollo crujiente y se ve que tiene mucha hambre.

Ángel responde:

—¡Sí!, tengo demasiada hambre. Me ha **convencido**, eso es lo que voy a **pedir**.

—**Perfecto,** ya lo **anoté**, y para los otros dos señores, ¿qué desean? —pregunta el encargado.

Armando se adelanta y dice:

—Yo sí voy a querer esa hamburguesa con pollo crujiente y además de eso me da un **extra** de **papas fritas**.

57. **Decisión:** Decision
58. **Convencido:** Convinced
59. **Pedir:** Order

60. **Perfecto**: Perfect
61. **Anoté:** I noted down
62. **Extra**: Extra
63. **Papas fritas:** French fries

—Yo quiero una hamburguesa **clásica**, no tengo mucha hambre —dice Frank.

—Listo, ya tomé su pedido. ¿Qué van a querer para tomar? —pregunta el encargado.

Frank responde:

—Tres refrescos, por favor.

Los tres amigos disfrutan de sus comidas y al finalizar, Frank llama a su amigo taxista para que los vaya a buscar y poder **dirigirse** a su casa, ya que sus amigos estaban **agotados** del viaje.

A la mañana siguiente, Ángel y Armando se despiertan y ven que Frank todavía seguía dormido. Por eso deciden salir de la casa a **desayunar** en el **cafetín** que se encontraba en la **esquina**.

64. **Clásica:** Classic
65. **Dirigirse:** To head for
66. **Agotados**: Exhausted
67. **Desayunar**: To have breakfast
68. **Cafetín:** Small café
69. **Esquina:** Corner

Al llegar, deciden pedir **empanadas**, que según los locales, eran las mejores que se podían encontrar en esa zona.

—Dos empanadas, una de **carne molida** y la otra de **puré de papas**, por favor —dice Ángel.

—Y a mí me da dos también, pero una de **camarones** y la otra me la da de **mariscos**. Para llevarme las dos de carne molida, por favor —dice Armando.

El que atiende el puesto de comida les dice:

—Aquí tienen, que disfruten de su desayuno, son $85.

Luego de **pagar** y de **disfrutar** de su desayuno, regresan al apartamento donde ya Frank estaba vestido esperándolos.

70. **Empanadas:** Empanadas
71. **Carne molida:** Ground beef
72. **Puré de papas:** Mashed potatoes
73. **Camarones**: Shrimp
74. **Mariscos:** Seafood
75. **Pagar**: To pay
76. **Disfrutar**: To enjoy

—¿Y mi comida?, quiero pensar que me trajeron desayuno —dice Frank **riéndose**.

—Claro, aquí está —dice Armando.

Pasan toda la mañana pensando qué van a hacer para la noche y a dónde van a ir a comer. Mientras deciden, van preparando y **salpimentando** la carne que había comprado Frank para la **parrilla**.

77. **Riéndose:** Laughing
78. **Salpimentando**: Spicing
79. **Parrilla:** Grill

Frank **se coloca** el **delantal** para comenzar a hacer la parrilla y entre el **humo** de los **carbones** comenta:

—En la noche vamos a ir a un lugar llamado «Qué Pinchos», donde nos vamos a comer unos **patacones** inmensos de **pernil**, no se van a arrepentir, es una de las **comidas rápidas** más famosas de la región.

—¿Cómo son esos patacones? —dice Ángel.

—Es una comida a base de **trozos aplanados** fritos de plátano verde o **maduro**, tradicional en la **culinaria** de varios países de América Latina y por supuesto de Maracaibo —explica Frank.

—Suena genial y muy delicioso —dice Armando.

—Y lo es, pero eso no es todo, **suele** hacerse cortando el plátano, verde o maduro, de forma **alargada**, **aplanando**, friendo y poniendo los **ingredientes** sobre él o entre dos plátanos

—sigue explicando emocionado Frank.

80. **Se coloca**: Puts on
81. **Delantal**: Apron
82. **Humo**: Smoke
83. **Carbones**: Coals
84. **Patacones**: Fried plantains
85. **Pernil:** Leg when speaking of food (in this case pork)
86. **Comidas rápidas:** Fast foods
87. **Trozos:** Pieces or bits
88. **Aplanados:** Flattened
89. **Maduro:** Ripe
90. **Culinaria**: Cuisine
91. **Suele:** Usually (used as an adverb)
92. **Alargada:** Long
93. **Aplanando:** Flattening
94. **Ingredientes**: Ingredients

Responde Ángel entre risas:

—Cálmate, sé que estás emocionado, pero en la noche vamos a ver qué tal son esos patacones que tú dices.

Los tres terminan la parrillada, llega la noche y Frank entusiasmado llama a su amigo taxista para que los busque y los lleve a «Qué Pinchos».

Una vez en el local, el mesero que ahí atiende, les pregunta:

—Muy buenas noches, caballeros, ¿para cuántas personas les gustaría la **mesa**?

—Mesa para tres, por favor —dice Frank emocionado.

Mientras se dirigían a la mesa, el mesero les pregunta:

—¿Quieren ver el menú o ya saben lo que van a pedir? Según sus caras, creo que ya sé lo que van a pedir.

—Pues claro, lo que todos vienen a comer aquí. ¿Me traes tres patacones **gratinados** y tres refrescos? —dice Frank.

95. **Mesa:** Table
96. **Gratinados:** Au gratin

—¿Gratinado? —preguntan Ángel y Armando.

—¡Sí!, aquí les colocan encima **queso** mozzarella y lo gratinan exponiendo la capa externa del patacón a una **fuente** intensa de calor con el **objeto** de que se ponga crujiente y **dorado**. ¡**DIVINO**! —responde Frank.

Al llegar los patacones a la mesa, Ángel y Armando estaban impresionados de lo grande que eran esos patacones.

—¿Vieron? Se ven **exquisitos**, ¡pruébenlos! —dice Frank.

Luego de dar el primer **mordisco** a ese patacón tan grande, dice Armando:

—Es increíble el sabor que deja en tu boca luego de mezclar el **queso derretido**, el pernil y lo crujiente del plátano. Esto está exquisito.

97. **Queso:** Cheese
98. **Fuente:** Source
99. **Objeto:** Objective
100. **Dorado:** Golden
101. **Divino:** Divine
102. **Exquisitos:** Exquisite
103. **Mordisco:** Bite
104. **Queso derretido:** Melted cheese

—¿Exquisito?, creo que es la comida rápida más deliciosa que he probado en mi vida. Definitivamente voy a aprender cómo hacer esto para poder hacerlo en mi casa —dice Ángel.

Frank no decía ninguna palabra, solo se limitaba a disfrutar de su comida y de escuchar a sus amigos, contento porque les había gustado eso que tenía guardado bajo la **manga**.

A Ángel y Armando, aún les quedaba poco menos de la **mitad** de su patacón. Ya no lo podían seguir comiendo, pero no querían detenerse ya que no querían parar de disfrutarlo.

Frank les comenta que pueden guardar y dejarlo para el desayuno, que eso es algo muy normal en las personas que viven en Maracaibo y sobre todo los que piden ese patacón.

Frank llama al mesero y le dice:

—¿Me coloca lo que dejaron mis compañeros en un **envase** para llevar y me trae la cuenta, por favor?

—Seguro, aquí tiene la cuenta, son $350, ¿cómo va a pagar? —pregunta el mesero.

—Pagaré con **tarjeta de crédito** —dice Frank.

—Perfecto, acompáñeme a la **caja registradora**, por favor —dice el mesero.

105. **Manga:** Sleeve
106. **Mitad:** Half
107. **Envase:** Container
108. **Tarjeta de crédito:** Credit card
109. **Caja registradora:** Cash register

Luego de pagar, se retiran de nuevo al apartamento. Nadie dijo ninguna palabra durante todo el camino, ya que todos estaban demasiado llenos.

Cuando llegan al apartamento, mientras Frank cerraba las **puertas**, sus amigos ya se habían quedado dormidos porque no podían más, quedar tan llenos les había agotado todas sus energías.

A la mañana siguiente, Frank fue el primero en despertarse esta vez. Mientras preparaba el café, se sonreía mientras veía a sus amigos llegar a la cocina con sus manos sobre el **estómago**.

110. **Puertas:** Doors
111. **Estómago:** Stomach

—¿Qué pasó, siguen con el estómago lleno aún? —dice Frank entre **carcajadas**

Ángel responde:

—No me importa, eso estaba demasiado delicioso, si es por mí vamos hoy también pero lastimosamente nos tenemos que regresar hoy.

—Pienso lo mismo que tú Ángel, pero definitivamente vamos a visitarlo de nuevo la próxima vez que vengamos a visitar a Frank —dice Armando.

—Sabía que les iba a encantar esa comida, es mi **lugar favorito** —dice Frank.

Terminan su café junto con sus desayunos y Frank, un poco **cabizbajo** porque ya sus amigos tienen que regresar a sus casas, llama a su amigo el taxista para que los busque.

Una vez en el aeropuerto, los tres grandes amigos, entre risas un poco llenas de **tristeza**, se despiden y se **prometen** que tarde o **temprano** se volverán a **reencontrar**.

112. **Carcajadas**: Loud bursts of laughter
113. **Lugar favorito:** Favourite place
114. **Cabizbajo**: Dejected/Sad
115. **Tristeza:** Sadness
116. **Prometen**: Promised
117. **Temprano**: Soon
118. **Reencontrar:** To meet again

EL AS BAJO LA MANGA
PREGUNTAS

1. ¿Dónde vive actualmente Frank?

    a. Lima

    b. Perú

    c. Maracaibo

2. ¿De dónde conoce Frank a Ángel y Armando?

    a. Del colegio

    b. De la universidad

    c. Del trabajo

3. ¿Cuándo fue la última vez que se vieron los tres amigos?

    a. Hace un año

    b. Hace diez años

    c. Hace dos años

4. ¿Quién hace la Parrilla?

    a. Frank

    b. Ángel

    c. Armando

5. ¿Qué pidieron en el último sitio de comida que visitaron?

    a. Patacón

    b. Doble hamburguesa de queso fundido

    c. Hamburguesa de pollo crujiente

EL AS BAJO LA MANGA
SOLUCIONES

1. C

2. A

3. C

4. A

5. A

EL AS BAJO LA MANGA
VOCABULARIO

1. **Graduado**: Graduate
2. **Periodista**: Journalist
3. **Actualmente**: Currently
4. **Viviendo**: Living
5. **Ciudad**: City
6. **Experimentando**: Experiencing
7. **Soltero**: Single
8. **Apartamento**: Apartment
9. **Estudio**: Studio
10. **Caracterizado**: Characterized
11. **Centro**: Center
12. **Atención**: Attention
13. **Presidente**: President
14. **Colegio**: School
15. **Sociedad**: Society
16. **Estudiantes**: Students
17. **Universidad**: College
18. **Emocionado**: Excited
19. **Mejores**: Best
20. **Semanas**: Weeks
21. **Vacaciones**: Vacation
22. **Ansioso**: Anxious
23. **Llegada**: Arrival
24. **Comprado**: Bought (verb: comprar)
25. **Siendo**: Being
26. **Visita**: Visit
27. **Aeropuerto**: Airport
28. **Pancarta**: Banner
29. **Mensaje**: Message
30. **Chistoso**: Funny
31. **Lejos**: Far
32. **Acercándose**: Approaching
33. **Rápido**: Quick
34. **Maletas**: Suitcases
35. **Como si fueran**: As if they were going to
36. **Quedarse**: To stay
37. **Verte**: To see you (verb: ver)
38. **Saludan**: Greet
39. **Abrazo**: Hug
40. **Tiempo**: Time
41. **Última**: Last
42. **Cumpleaños**: Birthday
43. **Conversar**: To converse
44. **Sillones**: Armchairs

45. **Muriendo de hambre**: Starving
46. **Comer:** To eat
47. **Puesto de comida callejera:** Street food stand
48. **Trayecto:** Journey
49. **Aeropuerto:** Airport
50. **Taxista**: Taxi driver
51. **Indecisos:** Undecided
52. **Delicioso:** Delicious
53. **Encargado**: Manager
54. **Bienvenidos:** Welcome
55. **Doble hamburguesa de queso fundido:** Double cheese burger
56. **Crujiente:** Crunchy
57. **Decisión:** Decision
58. **Convencido:** Convinced
59. **Pedir:** Order
60. **Perfecto**: Perfect
61. **Anoté:** I noted down
62. **Extra**: Extra
63. **Papas fritas:** French fries
64. **Clásica:** Classic
65. **Dirigirse:** To head for
66. **Agotados**: Exhausted
67. **Desayunar**: To have breakfast
68. **Cafetín:** Small café
69. **Esquina:** Corner
70. **Empanadas:** Empanadas
71. **Carne molida:** Ground beef
72. **Puré de papas:** Mashed potatoes
73. **Camarones**: Shrimp
74. **Mariscos:** Seafood
75. **Pagar**: To pay
76. **Disfrutar**: To enjoy
77. **Riéndose:** Laughing
78. **Salpimentando**: Spicing
79. **Parrilla:** Grill
80. **Se coloca**: Puts on
81. **Delantal**: Apron
82. **Humo**: Smoke
83. **Carbones**: Coals
84. **Patacones:** Fried plantains
85. **Pernil:** Leg when speaking of food (in this case pork)
86. **Comidas rápidas:** Fast foods
87. **Trozos:** Pieces or bits
88. **Aplanados:** Flattened

89. **Maduro:** Ripe
90. **Culinaria**: Cuisine
91. **Suele:** Usually (used as an adverb)
92. **Alargada:** Long
93. **Aplanando:** Flattening
94. **Ingredientes**: Ingredients
95. **Mesa:** Table
96. **Gratinados:** Au gratin
97. **Queso:** Cheese
98. **Fuente:** Source
99. **Objeto:** Objective
100. **Dorado:** Golden
101. **Divino:** Divine
102. **Exquisitos:** Exquisite
103. **Mordisco:** Bite
104. **Queso derretido:** Melted cheese
105. **Manga:** Sleeve
106. **Mitad:** Half
107. **Envase:** Container
108. **Tarjeta de crédito:** Credit card
109. **Caja registradora:** Cash register
110. **Puertas:** Doors
111. **Estómago:** Stomach
112. **Carcajadas**: Loud bursts of laughter
113. **Lugar favorito:** Favourite place
114. **Cabizbajo:** Dejected/Sad
115. **Tristeza:** Sadness
116. **Prometen**: Promised
117. **Temprano**: Soon
118. **Reencontrar:** To meet again

MERECIDAS VACACIONES
RESUMEN

Alejandro es un empresario muy ocupado que no ha tenido mucho tiempo para planificar unas vacaciones con su pareja Carol. Alejandro planifica, con la ayuda de un amable promotor de agencias de viaje, una maravillosa sorpresa para su pareja Carol, unas merecidas vacaciones en la playa. Estas vacaciones están llenas de sorpresas para Carol, desde una romántica cena en un yate privado, hasta un inesperado cambio de planes como lo es un viaje a un clima frio.

Alejandro is a very busy businessman who hasn't had much time to plan a vacation with his significant other Carol. Alejandro plans, with the help of a kind promoter of travel agencies, a wonderful surprise for his partner Carol, a well-deserved vacation at the beach. This holiday is full of surprises for Carol, from a romantic dinner on a private yacht, to an unexpected change of plans as it is a trip to a cold climate.

MERECIDAS VACACIONES

Alejandro, un **empresario** muy importante de la ciudad de Guadalajara, México, siempre muy **ocupado** con sus numerosas empresas, decide tomarse un **merecido descanso**.

Luego de hablar con su mano derecha, su **socio** José, decide tomar todos los días libres **acumulados** desde hace cinco años y así tomar unas largas vacaciones con su pareja Carol.

Alejandro, planea darle una **sorpresa** a Carol, ya que ella siempre ha querido irse de vacaciones junto a él, y él nunca había podido, así que **se dirige** a una **agencia de viajes**.

1. **Empresario:** Businessman
2. **Merecido:** Well deserved
3. **Descanso:** Break
4. **Socio:** Partner
5. **Acumulados:** Accumulated
6. **Sorpresa:** Surprise
7. **Se dirige:** Goes to
8. **Agencia de viajes:** Travel agency

Al llegar a la agencia es recibido por un cordial promotor y Alejandro le **plantea** su idea.

9. **Plantea:** Propose

—Necesito ayuda para planear mis vacaciones con mi pareja. Estas vacaciones serán una sorpresa para ella —dice Alejandro.

—Claro, ¿a dónde te **gustaría** llevarla para **sorprenderla**? —pregunta el promotor.

A lo que Alejandro responde:

—Aún no he decidido a dónde podríamos ir.

—¿Disfrutan de **climas cálidos** o fríos? —pregunta el promotor.

—He estado pensando que podríamos disfrutar de un **clima tropical**, en nuestros años de **relación** no hemos podidos **viajar** a lugares con ese clima —responde Alejandro.

10. **Gustaría:** Would like
11. **Sorprenderla:** Surprise her
12. **Climas cálidos:** Warm climates

13. **Clima tropical:** Tropical climate
14. **Relación:** Relationship
15. **Viajar:** To travel

—Tengo algunos **folletos** aquí que te gustaría mirar —le dice el promotor con la mejor intención de ayudarlo.

—¡Estos se ven **geniales**! —responde Alejandro al mirar los folletos.

—¿Sabes cuánto quieres **gastar** en estas vacaciones? —dice el promotor de la agencia de viajes.

—No tengo **límites**. Carol y yo nos **merecemos** estas vacaciones desde hace tiempo y no pienso **escatimar** —dice Alejandro decidido.

El promotor se ríe y responde:

—¡Así se habla! Bueno, toma estos folletos y vuelve a **consultarme** cuando quieras hacer tus **reservas**.

16. **Folletos:** Brochures
17. **Geniales:** Great
18. **Gastar:** To spend
19. **Límites:** Limits
20. **Merecemos:** We deserve
21. **Escatimar:** To skimp on
22. **Consultarme:** Consult me
23. **Reservas:** Reservations

Pasan los días y Alejando ve una y otra vez los folletos para tomar la decisión correcta y así **planificar** a la perfección las vacaciones tan **añoradas** de él y su pareja, así como también la sorpresa para Carol.

A la semana siguiente Alejandro toma la decisión y va hacia la agencia de viajes que había ido días atrás y le expresa al amable promotor su decisión.

—Un gusto volverlo a ver, señor Alejandro, ¿ya tiene tomada su decisión? —pregunta el promotor.

—El gusto es mío, pues sí, ya he tomado la **decisión**. Después de ver una y otra vez los folletos tengo mi **destino** —responde Alejandro.

—Me alegro que le hayan servido, dígame ¿cuál será su destino? —dice el promotor.

—He **escogido** Acapulco, acá mismo en México —responde Alejandro.

—Muy buena **elección,** señor Alejandro, es bueno conocer cada rincón de su **país** —acota el promotor.

—¿Podrías ayudarme a hacer una reservación de avión? —pregunta Alejandro.

—Estaré encantado de ayudarlo. Buscaré las próximas **fechas disponibles** —dice el promotor.

24. **Planificar:** To plan
25. **Añoradas:** Longed for
26. **Decisión:** Decision
27. **Destino:** Destination
28. **Escogido:** Selected
29. **Elección:** Choice
30. **País:** Country
31. **Fechas disponibles:** Available dates

El promotor busca en su computadora las próximas fechas disponibles para el viaje a Acapulco que Alejandro quería como sorpresa para Carol. Cuando encuentra la fecha más próxima dice:

—Hay un **vuelo** disponible para esta misma **semana**, ¿le gustaría esa fecha?

—¡Sí!, Claro que me gustaría, mientras más próximo sea mejor, ya que no puedo aguantarme las **ganas** de contarle de las vacaciones a Carol —responde Alejandro muy entusiasmado.

—¡Listo! Ya tiene hecha su **reservación** en el vuelo de este fin de semana a primera hora de la **mañana** —dice el promotor.

—Muchísimas gracias, me encantó tu buen **trato** —dice Alejandro—, ¿también puedes ayudarme con la reservación del hotel?

—Claro que sí, le haré la reserva en el mejor **hotel** de la zona, donde tiene todo incluido, incluso un paseo en un **yate privado** con una cena para dos —responde el promotor.

32. **Vuelo:** Flight
33. **Semana:** Week
34. **Ganas:** Desire
35. **Reservación:** Reservation
36. **Mañana:** Morning
37. **Trato:** Treatment
38. **Hotel:** Hotel
39. **Yate privado:** Private yacht

—Me encanta la idea, has sido de mucha ayuda para la planificación de estas esperadas vacaciones. Quién sabe si desde Acapulco te llame para hacer otras reservas —dice Alejandro muy agradecido.

El promotor le entrega a Alejandro sus dos **boletos**, más la reserva del hotel en Acapulco. Alejandro se dirige al **apartamento** de Carol para darle la sorpresa.

Al llegar al apartamento de Carol, Alejandro muy entusiasmado **coloca** los boletos en su cama y la **engaña** diciendo que son unos papeles del trabajo que quiere que revise.

40. **Boletos:** Tickets
41. **Apartamento:** Apartment
42. **Coloca:** Places
43. **Engaña:** Deceives

Carol, al tomarlos de la **cama** y abrirlos, coloca cara de **confusión** y le pregunta a Alejandro:

—No entiendo amor, ¿qué es esto?"

—Lee bien de qué **se trata** y **verás** —responde Alejandro con tono misterioso y **jocoso**.

Asombrada, Carol lee una y otra vez los papeles que Alejandro le había puesto en la cama y exclama:

—¡No lo puedo creer! ¿Iremos de vacaciones a Acapulco?

—Sí, al fin tendremos nuestras **merecidas** vacaciones y tienes que empezar a **empacar**, ya que son este **fin de semana** — le dice Alejandro a Carol con mucha felicidad.

44. **Cama:** Bed
45. **Confusión:** Confusion
46. **Se Trata:** It is about
47. **Verás:** You will see
48. **Jocoso:** Humorous
49. **Asombrada:** Astonished
50. **Merecidas:** Deserved
51. **Empacar:** To pack
52. **Fin de semana:** Weekend

Carol, muy alegre, salta a darle un gran abrazo a Alejandro y corre a su **armario** para preparar sus **maletas** con los mejores y más bonitos **trajes de baño** que ella tiene.

Empieza a **preparar** sus maletas y Alejandro se asombra de todo lo que quiere llevar, desde grandes **sombreros**, hasta variados **lentes** de diferentes colores y formas que combinan con cada uno de los trajes de baño que lleva.

Llegado el día, Alejandro y Carol llaman a un taxi y suben su **equipaje** al carro para ir rumbo al **Aeropuerto** Internacional de Guadalajara Miguel Hidalgo y Costilla. Una vez en el aeropuerto, luego de haber **chequeado** su equipaje, suben al **avión** y parten a Acapulco.

Al **desembarcar** del avión y tomar sus equipajes, son esperados por un **chofer** que tiene en su mano un pequeño **cartel** con sus nombres.

53. **Armario:** Closet
54. **Maletas:** Suitcases
55. **Trajes de baños:** Bathing suits
56. **Preparar:** To prepare
57. **Sombreros:** Hats
58. **Lentes:** Glasses
59. **Equipaje:** Luggage
60. **Aeropuerto:** Airport
61. **Chequeado:** Checked
62. **Avión:** Airplane
63. **Desembarcar:** To get off
64. **Chofer:** Driver
65. **Cartel:** Poster

Asombrados por el hecho, Alejandro y Carol se acercan a él y le dicen:

—Buenos días, señor, disculpe pero no hemos **contratado** ningún **servicio** de **transporte**.

—Buenos días, señor y señora, este servicio es parte de la reserva del hotel. ¿Puedo tomar sus equipajes y **llevarlos**? —dice el chofer con mucha cordialidad.

—¡Qué bien! No sabía que esa reserva **incluía** este servicio. Claro, sería un placer que nos llevara al hotel —dice Alejandro entusiasmado por la atención del chofer y la calidad del hotel hacia donde se dirigían.

Se suben a la **camioneta** identificada con el nombre del hotel y toman una **autopista** llena de grandes **palmeras** en ambos lados. Apreciando el paisaje, se les hace muy rápido el viaje de una hora desde el aeropuerto hasta el hotel.

66. **Contratado:** Hired
67. **Servicio:** Service
68. **Transporte:** Transport
69. **Llevarlos:** Take them
70. **Incluía:** It included
71. **Camioneta:** Van
72. **Autopista:** Freeway
73. **Palmeras:** Palms

Una vez en la **entrada principal** del hotel, Alejandro y Carol son **recibidos** por una hermosa chica que les ofrece unas **refrescantes** bebidas y los saluda cordialmente:

—Buenos días, señor Alejandro y señora Carol, sean bienvenidos a Acapulco, espero disfruten cada segundo de su **estadía** en este maravilloso **paraíso tropical**.

74. **Entrada Principal:** Main entrance
75. **Refrescantes:** Refreshing
76. **Estadía:** Stay
77. **Paraíso:** Paradise
78. **Tropical:** Tropical

Anonadados porque sabía sus nombres, se alegran y dicen entre ellos que estas serán las **mejores** vacaciones de sus vidas.

Rápidamente suben a su amplia y linda **habitación** con una gran **vista** a la **playa** y se colocan sus trajes de baño para no perder ni un minuto de tiempo disfrutando las vacaciones.

Al ir a la playa, escogen la mejor **ubicación**, una **mesa** en la **arena** con una enorme **sombrilla** y dos cómodas **sillas plegables**. Alejandro y Carol disfrutan de su día de **sol** hasta la hora del **almuerzo** y van al restaurante de la playa del hotel.

79. **Anonadados**: Astonished
80. **Mejores:** Top
81. **Habitación:** Room
82. **Vista:** View
83. **Playa:** Beach
84. **Ubicación:** Location
85. **Mesa:** Table
86. **Arena:** Sand
87. **Sombrilla:** Umbrella
88. **Sillas plegables:** Folding chairs
89. **Sol:** Sun
90. **Almuerzo:** Lunch

Son atendidos por un **mesonero** muy alegre que les ofrece el **plato especial** del restaurante, un enorme **pescado frito**, con **camarones rebosados**, acompañado de unas suculentas **papas fritas**.

Llega el enorme plato a la mesa de Alejandro y Carol y quedan extasiados por lo buena que se ve la comida, y el mesonero les dice:

—Disfruten de su comida, espero que les quede espacio para la **cena romántica**.

Por lo que Carol se asombra y le pregunta a Alejandro:

—¿También me sorprenderás con una cena romántica en la playa?

—Y no solo eso, será en un **yate** —responde Alejandro.

91. **Mesonero:** Innkeeper
92. **Plato especial:** Special dish
93. **Pescado frito:** Fried fish
94. **Camarones rebozados:** Butter coated shrimp
95. **Papas fritas:** French fries
96. **Cena romántica:** Romantic dinner
97. **Yate:** Yacht

Llegada la noche, Alejandro y Carol se colocan su mejor **vestimenta playera** y suben al yate en espera de la cena romántica a la luz de la **luna**, y Carol dice:

—Este viaje ha sido el mejor de mi vida, gracias por cada detalle.

—El mío también, nos lo tenemos muy bien merecido. Ya que pasamos cinco años sin poder viajar. Además, estas vacaciones no terminan aquí, mañana en la mañana te sorprenderé

—le dice Alejandro a Carol.

Amanece en Acapulco y lo primero que Alejandro hace es **llamar** a aquel promotor de la agencia de viajes que le reservó sus boletos.

98. **Vestimenta playera:** Beachwear
99. **Luna:** Moon
100. **Amanece:** The sun rises
101. **Llamar:** To call

—¿Cómo está, señor Alejandro?, ¿cómo ha pasado sus días en la playa? —pregunta el promotor al ver que lo llamaba Alejandro.

—Excelente, gracias por ayudarme a tomar esta decisión, pero quiero que me ayudes a seguir sorprendiendo a Carol. Ahora quiero un viaje a un **clima frío** y **fuera** de México —dice Alejandro.

—Por supuesto que lo ayudaré, le encontraré un vuelo a Bariloche en el país de Argentina. Así podrán disfrutar de un clima muy frío después de unos días al sol. Se irán **directamente** desde Acapulco —le responde el promotor.

102. **Clima Frío:** Cold weather
103. **Fuera:** Outside
104. **Directamente:** Directly

Al finalizar la llamada, Alejandro **despierta** amorosamente a Carol y le dice:

—Despierta, mi amor, tenemos que empacar y comprar unos **abrigos**, porque nos vamos a Bariloche, Argentina.

Carol salta de la emoción y le dice a Alejandro:

—No lo puedo **creer**, has planificado las vacaciones **perfectas**. De ahora en adelante todos los años tenemos que planificar **escapadas** como estas.

Ambos se fueron en el próximo vuelo desde Acapulco a Argentina y al finalizar sus vacaciones, prometieron que cada año viajarían a un lugar distinto.

105. **Despierta:** Awakes
106. **Abrigos:** Coats
107. **Creer:** To believe
108. **Perfectas:** Perfect
109. **Escapadas:** Getaways

MERECIDAS VACACIONES
PREGUNTAS

1. **¿Por qué Alejandro no tomaba vacaciones?**

   a. Porque estaba ocupado con sus numerosas empresas.

   b. Porque su pareja no quería vacaciones junto a él.

   c. Porque escatimaba en gastos.

2. **¿Adónde le gustaría viajar a Alejandro por primera vez?**

   a. Clima cálido.

   b. Clima frío.

   c. Clima tropical.

3. **¿Cuál es el primer destino de Alejandro y Carol?**

   a. Bariloche.

   b. Acapulco.

   c. Guadalajara.

4. **¿Dónde es la cena romántica?**

   a. En un avión.

   b. En un yate privado.

   c. En el restaurante de la playa.

5. **¿Qué clima le gustaría a Alejandro para su próximo destino?**

   a. Clima tropical.

   b. Clima cálido.

   c. Clima frío.

MERECIDAS VACACIONES
SOLUCIONES

1. A

2. C

3. B

4. B

5. C

MERECIDAS VACACIONES
VOCABULARIO

1. **Empresario:** Businessman
2. **Merecido:** Well deserved
3. **Descanso:** Break
4. **Socio:** Partner
5. **Acumulados:** Accumulated
6. **Sorpresa:** Surprise
7. **Se dirige:** Goes to
8. **Agencia de viajes:** Travel agency
9. **Plantea:** Proposes
10. **Gustaría:** Would like
11. **Sorprenderla:** Surprise her
12. **Climas cálidos:** Warm climates
13. **Clima tropical:** Tropical climate
14. **Relación:** Relationship
15. **Viajar:** To travel
16. **Folletos:** Brochures
17. **Geniales:** Great
18. **Gastar:** To spend
19. **Límites:** Limits
20. **Merecemos:** We deserve
21. **Escatimar:** To skimp on
22. **Consultarme:** Consult me
23. **Reserva:** Reservations
24. **Planificar:** To plan
25. **Añoradas:** Longed for
26. **Decisión:** Decision
27. **Destino:** Destination
28. **Escogido:** Selected
29. **Elección:** Choice
30. **País:** Country
31. **Fechas disponibles:** Available dates
32. **Vuelo:** Flight
33. **Semana:** Week
34. **Ganas:** Desire
35. **Reservación:** Reservation
36. **Mañana:** Morning
37. **Trato:** Treatment
38. **Hotel:** Hotel
39. **Yate privado:** Private yacht
40. **Boletos:** Tickets

41. **Apartamento:** Apartment

42. **Coloca:** Place

43. **Engaña:** Deceives

44. **Cama:** Bed

45. **Confusión:** Confusion

46. **Se Trata:** It is about

47. **Verás:** You will see

48. **Jocoso:** Humorous

49. **Asombrada:** Astonished

50. **Merecidas:** Deserved

51. **Empacar:** Pack

52. **Fin de semana:** Weekend

53. **Armario:** Closet

54. **Maletas:** Suitcases

55. **Trajes de baños:** Bathing suits

56. **Preparar:** To prepare

57. **Sombreros:** Hats

58. **Lentes:** Glasses

59. **Equipaje:** Luggage

60. **Aeropuerto:** Airport

61. **Chequeado:** Checked

62. **Avión:** Airplane

63. **Desembarcar:** To get off

64. **Chofer:** Driver

65. **Cartel:** Poster

66. **Contratado:** Hired

67. **Servicio:** Service

68. **Transporte:** Transport

69. **Llevarlos:** Take them

70. **Incluía:** It included

71. **Camioneta:** Van

72. **Autopista:** Freeway

73. **Palmeras:** Palms

74. **Entrada principal:** Main entrance

75. **Refrescantes:** Refreshing

76. **Estadía:** Stay

77. **Paraíso:** Paradise

78. **Tropical:** Tropical

79. **Mejores:** Top

80. **Habitación:** Room

81. **Vista:** View

82. **Playa:** Beach

83. **Ubicación:** Location

84. **Mesa:** Table

85. **Arena:** Sand

86. **Sombrilla:** Umbrella

87. **Sillas plegables:** Folding chairs

88. **Sol:** Sun

89. **Almuerzo:** Lunch

90. **Mesonero:** Innkeeper

91. **Plato especial:** Special dish

92. **Pescado frito:** Fried fish

93. **Camarones rebosados:** Butter coated shrimp
94. **Papas fritas:** French fries
95. **Cena romántica:** Romantic dinner
96. **Yate:** Yacht
97. **Vestimenta playera:** Beachwear
98. **Luna:** Moon
99. **Amanece:** The sun rises
100. **Llamar:** To call
101. **Clima frío:** Cold weather
102. **Fuera:** Outside
103. **Directamente:** Directly
104. **Despierta:** Awakes
105. **Abrigos:** Coats
106. **Creer:** To believe
107. **Perfectas:** Perfect
108. **Escapadas:** Getaways

ATAJOS SECRETOS
RESUMEN

Elena es una administradora de cuarenta y dos años de Montevideo, Uruguay, que ha dedicado su vida al trabajo, no tiene hijos, pero tiene dos sobrinos de su hermana Elisa, con los cuales comparte un día a la semana, todo el día, despejándose de su trabajo. Elena, para poder llegar a su oficina, la cual queda en el centro de la ciudad, puede tomar un taxi o el autobús, todo esto dependiendo del tráfico de la ciudad y la hora de llegada al lugar. Cada vez que hay un embotellamiento, Elena ayuda al chofer del taxi con un atajo secreto.

Elena is a 42-year-old administrator from Montevideo, Uruguay, who has dedicated her life to work, has no children, but has a nephew and a niece of her sister Elisa, with whom she shares one day a week, all day, clearing herself of her work. Elena, to get to her office, which is in the center of the city, can take a taxi or the bus, all this depending on the traffic of the city and the time of arrival at the place. Every time there is a traffic jam, Elena helps the taxi driver with a secret shortcut.

ATAJOS SECRETOS

Elena es una profesional de la **administración** de cuarenta y dos años, que vive en Montevideo, capital de Uruguay.

Ella no se ha casado, ni ha tenido hijos ya que es una **adicta al trabajo**. Todos los días, a toda hora mira su **celular** y su tableta esperando **mensajes** de su oficina.

La oficina de Elena está **ubicada** en la parte más central de la ciudad de Montevideo. Desde su casa hasta la oficina, Elena tarda cuarenta y cinco minutos en carro y una hora en **autobús**, todo esto dependiendo de cómo esté el tráfico de la ciudad.

1. **Administración:** administration
2. **Adicta al trabajo:** workaholic
3. **Celular:** Cell phone
4. **Mensajes:** Messages
5. **Ubicada:** Located
6. **Autobús:** Bus

Elena tiene dos **sobrinos**, Jennifer y Juan Carlos, **ambos** hijos de su hermana Elisa. Jennifer tiene cinco años y **asiste** a un **preescolar**. Juan Carlos tiene ocho y va a clases en una **escuela cercana** a la oficina de Jennifer.

Un día a la semana, Elena deja a un lado su teléfono y su tableta para pasar el día con sus sobrinos. Los **busca** en el preescolar y la escuela y los **lleva** de **paseo** a **parques** cercanos.

7. **Sobrinos:** Nieces and nephews
8. **Ambos:** Both of them
9. **Asiste:** Attends (asistir a)
10. **Preescolar:** Preschool
11. **Escuela:** School
12. **Cercana:** Close
13. **Busca:** Search
14. **Lleva:** To take
15. **Paseo:** Walk
16. **Parques:** Parks

Un día normal de Elena **comienza** con un buen café, unas ricas **tostadas francesas** y **se alista** para un nuevo día de trabajo. Al terminar de vestirse, Elena llama desde su celular a un taxi, ya que esperar el **transporte público** de la ciudad lleva mucho tiempo.

Al escuchar la **bocina** del taxi, Elena baja de su **apartamento** y s**e sube** al **carro**.

—Buenos días, señorita —dice el **taxista** con mucha amabilidad.

—Buenos días, señor. ¿Cómo **amanece** hoy? —responde Elena al chofer del taxi.

—Muy bien, gracias. ¿Hacia dónde se **dirige** hoy? —pregunta el taxista.

17. **Comienza:** Begins
18. **Tostadas francesas:** French toast
19. **Se alista:** Gets ready
20. **Transporte público:** Public transport
21. **Bocina:** Horn
22. **Apartamento:** Apartment
23. **Se sube:** Gets in (a vehicle)
24. **Carro:** Car
25. **Taxista:** Cabbie/Taxi driver
26. **Amanece:** The sun rises
27. **Se dirige:** Goes to

—Voy hacia mi trabajo que queda en el centro de la ciudad —responde Elena.

—Está bien, voy a tratar de tomar una **ruta despejada**, ya que a esta hora hay mucho **tráfico** —acota el chofer del taxi.

—Sí, me pasa todos los días, pero de tanto que he pasado por esta **vía**, sé de muchas **vías alternas** que nos van a ayudar a **escapar** del **caótico** tráfico de la ciudad —responde Elena.

28. **Ruta despejada:** Clear route

29. **Tráfico:** Traffic

30. **Vía:** Route

31. **Vías alternas:** Alternate ways

32. **Escapar:** Escape

33. **Caótico:** Chaotic

El chofer toma la ruta que piensa que está más despejada, pero sin ellos saber que pocas calles más adelante **se encuentran con** un **embotellamiento** gigante, los carros no pueden pasarse a un **carril** diferente y se ve que están todos **atascados**.

Elena se da cuenta rápidamente y le exclama al chofer del taxi:

—¡No siga hacia **adelante**! —Dice Elena con rapidez—. **Gire** hacia la **derecha**, y en dos calles más adelante encontraremos un pequeño **callejón** que nos lleva justo detrás de mi oficina.

34. **Se encuentran con:** They run into

35. **Embotellamiento:** Traffic jam

36. **Carril:** Lane

37. **Atascados:** Stuck

38. **Adelante:** Ahead

39. **Gire:** Turn

40. **Derecha:** Right

41. **Callejón:** Alley

—¿Está segura? —Pregunta el chofer desconfiado—. Quizás por esas calles también esté el tráfico **colapsado**.

—Estoy muy segura, ya verá que vamos a llegar en muy poco tiempo —responde Elena muy segura de sus palabras.

El chofer le **hace caso** a Elena y toma la ruta recomendada por ella, gira a la derecha y al encontrar el pequeño callejón que Elena había mencionado, se da cuenta que ella tiene razón y dice:

—¡**Impresionante**! Tardamos muy poco, usted sí que sabe de rutas alternas, se merece un **descuento** en la **tarifa**.

42. **Colapsado:** Blocked
43. **Hace caso:** Obeys
44. **Impresionante:** Awesome
45. **Descuento:** Discount
46. **Tarifa:** Rate

A lo que Elena responde sonrojada:

—No se preocupe, no me ha costado nada decirle mis pequeños **atajos secretos**.

—¡Y muy secretos! En mis años de experiencia como **taxista** nunca me había tardado menos de cuarenta y cinco minutos en esta ruta y hoy solo nos hemos tardado treinta minutos, no puedo creerlo —exclama el taxista todavía impresionado.

El chofer deja a Elena en frente de la puerta de su oficina y le dice:

—¡Que tenga un lindo día!; **estoy a la orden** cuando necesite un servicio de taxi y así poder conocer muchos de sus **caminos** secretos.

—Muy amable, estoy segura que lo volveré a llamar, que usted también tenga un lindo día y que el tráfico **sea** muy **fluido** hoy —responde Elena al taxista.

47. **Atajos secretos:** Secret shortcuts

48. **Taxista:** Taxi driver

49. **Estoy a la orden:** I'm at your service

50. **Caminos:** Roads

51. **Sea:** To be (subjunctive form of ser)

52. **Fluido:** Fluid

Al llegar a su oficina, Elena se sienta en su **escritorio** y comienza a trabajar como **diariamente** lo hace, **sin parar ni un minuto**, entre su celular, su computadora y su tableta, se pasan las horas de trabajo muy rápido.

Y cuando **menos se lo espera**, **finaliza** la **jornada de trabajo** y llega la hora de ir de nuevo a su apartamento.

53. **Escritorio:** Desk

54. **Diariamente:** Daily

55. **Sin parar ni un minuto:** Not stoping for even one minute

56. **Menos se los espera:** Least expected

57. **Finaliza:** Brings to an end

58. **Jornada de trabajo:** Working day

Como no está **apurada** en llegar, Elena decide tomar el transporte público, y se dirige a la **parada** más cercana de autobús. Esperando el autobús, recibe una llamada a su celular de su hermana Elisa. Contesta el teléfono celular y escucha:

—Hola, Elena ¿Cómo estás?

—Bien, ¿y tú?, ¿cómo están mis sobrinos? —pregunta Elena.

—Todos estamos muy bien, gracias. Te llamaba para pedirte un favor, ¿estás **desocupada**? —dice Elisa.

—Sí, **casualmente** espero el **próximo** autobús para ir a mi apartamento, ¿qué necesitas? —dice Elena.

—Tengo una **reunión** la noche de hoy y no tengo **con quién** dejar a Jennifer y Juan Carlos, pensaba que podrías **cuidarlos** y que hoy podría ser tu día con ellos —responde Elisa.

59. **Apurada:** Hurried
60. **Parada:** Stop (noun)
61. **Desocupada:** Unoccupied
62. **Casualmente:** Casually
63. **Próximo:** Next
64. **Reunión:** Meeting
65. **Con quién:** With whom
66. **Cuidarlos:** Take care of them (verb: cuidar)

—Por supuesto que puedo cuidarlos, ya busco un taxi y voy a tu casa para **buscarlos** —dice Elena muy emocionada porque va a ver a sus sobrinos.

Elena camina fuera de la parada de autobús y llama a un taxi con un **estruendoso silbido**. El taxi más cercano se **acerca** a la **acera** y ella se sube al carro amarillo **típico**.

—Buenas tardes, señor, necesito dirigirme a la **urbanización** La Capital; en la calle principal —dice Elena explicando la **dirección**.

67. **Buscarlos:** Look for them (verb: buscar)
68. **Estruendoso:** Thunderous
69. **Silbido:** Whistle
70. **Acerca:** About
71. **Acera:** Sidewalk
72. **Típico:** Typical
73. **Urbanización:** Housing development
74. **Dirección:** Address

—Buenas tardes, señorita. Está bien, se dónde queda ubicada esa urbanización, llegaremos lo más pronto posible —responde el taxista amablemente.

Al pasar por unas cuantas calles, **semáforos** e **intersecciones**, Elena muy confundida por no saber dónde está, le pregunta al taxista:

—Señor, ¿sabe usted hacia dónde se dirige? Veo que va en dirección contraria a mi **destino**.

—Sí señorita —responde el taxista con mucha seguridad—. He tomado estas vías un par de veces y aunque estemos en **sentido contrario** a su destino, llegaremos muy rápido a él.

75. **Semáforos:** Traffic lights
76. **Intersecciones:** Intersections
77. **Destino:** Destination
78. **Sentido contrario:** Wrong way

—**Confiaré** en su experiencia —dice Elena todavía un poco confundida.

Elena, un poco **mareada** de todas las **vueltas** que ha dado con el taxista, al fin se encuentra ubicada en la urbanización donde está la casa de su hermana y le describe la **fachada** de la casa al taxista para que no haya ninguna otra **confusión**.

—Al doblar a la izquierda, verá una casa muy grande de **color** blanco con **ventanas** azules, es ahí a donde voy —acota Elena al chofer del taxi.

—Está bien, señorita, ¿quiere que espere por usted o llamará a otra **unidad** de taxi? —dice el chofer.

79. **Confiaré:** I will trust

80. **Mareada:** Dizzy

81. **Vueltas:** Turns

82. **Fachada:** Facade

83. **Confusión:** Confusion

84. **Color:** Color

85. **Ventanas:** Windows

86. **Unidad:** Unit

—Sí, necesito que me espere, busco a mis sobrinos y regreso en un momento —responde Elena.

Al **bajarse** del auto, Elena camina a paso rápido desde la calle hasta la puerta de la casa de su hermana Elisa y escucha desde **lejos** las voces de sus dos sobrinos Jennifer y Juan Carlos muy alegres.

—¡Tía, tía, llegaste! —exclama Jennifer y Juan Carlos al mismo tiempo.

—¿Están listos para una noche de **pijamas** muy divertida? —pregunta Elena muy emocionada.

A lo que Jennifer y Juan Carlos responden exclamando:

—Sí tía, estamos muy emocionados de pasar la noche en tu casa.

87. **Bajarse:** Gets out of a car

88. **Lejos:** Far

89. **Pijamas:** Pajamas

—Yo también estoy muy emocionada; mejor **apúrense** que hay un taxi **esperando** en **frente** de la casa.

Los sobrinos de Elena, **recogen** sus bolsos del **suelo**, se **despiden** de su mamá Elisa y corren a ver quién llega primero a la **puerta trasera** del taxi. Juan Carlos **ganándo**le la **carrera** a su hermana menor Jennifer, decide que él irá entre su tía y ella para así ver toda la ruta.

90. **Apúrense:** Hurry up
91. **Esperando:** Waiting
92. **Frente:** Front
93. **Recogen:** Pick up
94. **Suelo:** Ground
95. **Despiden:** Say goodbye
96. **Puerta trasera:** Back door
97. **Ganando:** Winning
98. **Carrera:** Race

Cae la noche de camino a la casa de Elena y las luces de los carros en la **autopista alumbran** todo el paisaje.

Al llegar a casa de Elena, sus sobrinos planean las **actividades** que harán con su tía antes de ir a dormir. Desde una deliciosa cena llena de dulces, hasta ver películas animadas, por lo que Elena exclama:

—Niños, igual tienen que dormirse muy **temprano**. Mañana los voy a llevar a sus respectivas escuelas y después iremos al parque de la **esquina**. Así es que ¡tienen que guardar energías para mañana!

99. **Autopista:** Freeway
100. **Alumbran:** Illuminate
101. **Actividades:** Activities
102. **Temprano:** Early
103. **Esquina:** Corner

Jennifer y Juan Carlos muy emocionados porque pasarán otro día con su tía Elena, cenan junto a ella y se van a la cama muy temprano.

Pasada la noche, Elena despierta a sus sobrinos con un **delicioso desayuno**, tostadas francesas, y como es de costumbre, llama a un taxi desde su celular para empezar su día.

Sin esperarlo, se da cuenta que el taxi que la espera, es el **mismo** taxista que el día anterior la llevó a su oficina. Al subirse al carro el chofer le pregunta:

104. Delicioso desayuno: Delicious breakfast

105. Mismo: Same

—Buenos días, señorita, ¿se dirige a su oficina en el centro de la ciudad?

—¡Hola!, esta vez nos dirigimos a las escuelas de mis sobrinos, es por la misma ruta para llegar a mi oficina —responde Elena.

—Está bien, espero que para este camino también tenga un gran atajo y así aprender algo nuevo —dice entre risas el chofer.

—También lo tengo y no dudaré en decírselo si es para llegar a **buena hora** —responde Elena, riéndose también.

El chofer del taxi, toma la misma ruta que tomó para dejar a Elena el día anterior en su oficina, y como era de esperar necesitó de los atajos secretos de Elena para llegar a la hora a las escuelas de sus sobrinos, por el **tráfico pesado** del centro de Montevideo.

106. Buena hora: Good time

107. Tráfico pesado: Heavy traffic

ATAJOS SECRETOS
PREGUNTAS

1. **¿Por qué Elena le pide al chofer que no siga hacia adelante?**
   a. Porque hay un embotellamiento gigante
   b. Porque la ruta está despejada
   c. Porque quiere hacer tiempo antes de llegar al trabajo

2. **¿Por qué el chofer del taxi está impresionado?**
   a. Por el tráfico caótico
   b. Por las condiciones de la ruta
   c. Por los atajos secretos que sabe Elena

3. **¿Por qué Elena decide tomar el transporte público?**
   a. Porque está apurada
   b. Porque no está apurada
   c. Porque quiere buscar a sus sobrinos

4. **¿Cómo busca Elena a sus sobrinos?**
   a. En taxi
   b. En autobús
   c. En su carro

5. **¿Hacia dónde se dirige Elena con sus sobrinos en la mañana?**
   a. Para su apartamento
   b. Para su oficina
   c. Para sus respectivas escuelas

ATAJOS SECRETOS
SOLUCIONES

1. A

2. C

3. B

4. A

5. C

ATAJOS SECRETOS
VOCABULARIO

1. **Administración:** administration
2. **Adicta al trabajo:** workaholic
3. **Celular:** Cell pone
4. **Mensajes:** Messages
5. **Ubicada:** Located
6. **Autobús:** Bus
7. **Sobrinos:** Nieces and nephews
8. **Ambos:** Both
9. **Asiste:** Attends (asistir a)
10. **Preescolar:** Preschool
11. **Escuela:** School
12. **Cercana:** Close
13. **Busca:** Searches
14. **Lleva:** Takes
15. **Paseo:** Walk
16. **Parques:** Parks
17. **Comienza:** Begins
18. **Tostadas francesas:** French toast
19. **Se alista:** Get ready
20. **Transporte público:** Public transport
21. **Bocina:** Horn
22. **Apartamento:** Apartment
23. **Se sube:** Gets in (a vehicle)
24. **Carro:** Car
25. **Taxista:** Cabbie/Taxi driver
26. **Amanece:** The sun rises
27. **Se dirige:** Runs/Goes to
28. **Ruta despejada:** Clear route
29. **Tráfico:** Traffic
30. **Vía:** Route
31. **Vías alternas:** Alternate ways
32. **Escapar:** Escape
33. **Caótico:** Chaotic
34. **Se encuentran con:** They run into
35. **Embotellamiento:** Traffic jam
36. **Carril:** Lane
37. **Atascados:** Stuck
38. **Adelante:** Ahead
39. **Gire:** Turn

40. **Derecha:** Right
41. **Callejón:** Alley
42. **Colapsado:** Blocked
43. **Hace caso:** Obeys
44. **Impresionante:** Awesome
45. **Descuento:** Discount
46. **Tarifa:** Rate
47. **Atajos secretos:** Secret shortcuts
48. **Taxista:** Taxi driver/Cabbie
49. **Estoy a la orden:** I'm at your service
50. **Caminos:** Roads
51. **Sea:** To be (subjunctive form of ser)
52. **Fluido:** Fluid
53. **Escritorio:** Desk
54. **Diariamente:** Daily
55. **Sin parar ni un minuto:** Not stoping for even one minute
56. **Menos se lo espera:** Least expected
57. **Finaliza:** Brings to an end
58. **Jornada de trabajo:** Working day
59. **Apurada:** Hurried
60. **Parada:** Stop (noun)
61. **Desocupada:** Unoccupied
62. **Casualmente:** Casually
63. **Próximo:** Next
64. **Reunión:** Meeting
65. **Con quién:** With whom
66. **Cuidarlos:** Take care of them (verb: cuidar)
67. **Buscarlos:** Look for them (verb: buscar)
68. **Estruendoso:** Thunderous
69. **Silbido:** Whistle
70. **Acerca:** About
71. **Acera:** Sidewalk
72. **Típico:** Typical
73. **Urbanización:** Housing development
74. **Dirección:** Address
75. **Semáforos:** Traffic lights
76. **Intersecciones:** Intersections
77. **Destino:** Destination
78. **Sentido contrario:** Wrong way
79. **Confiaré:** I will trust
80. **Mareada:** Dizzy
81. **Vueltas:** Turns

82. **Fachada:** Facade

83. **Confusión:** Confusion

84. **Color:** Color

85. **Ventanas:** Windows

86. **Unidad:** Unity

87. **Bajarse:** Gets out of a car

88. **Lejos:** Far

89. **Pijamas:** Pajamas

90. **Apúrense:** Hurry up

91. **Esperando:** Waiting

92. **Frente:** Front

93. **Recogen:** Pick up

94. **Suelo:** Ground

95. **Despiden:** To say goodbye

96. **Puerta trasera:** Back door

97. **Ganando:** Winning

98. **Carrera:** Race

99. **Autopista:** Freeway

100. **Alumbran:** To illuminate

101. **Actividades:** Activities

102. **Temprano:** Early

103. **Esquina:** Corner

104. **Delicioso desayuno:** Delicious breakfast

105. **Mismo:** Same

106. **Buena hora:** Good time

107. **Tráfico pesado:** Heavy traffic

GRANJA LOS VILLALOBOS
RESUMEN

Los Villalobos es una familia de cuatro integrantes, que viven en una granja en las afueras de Costa Rica. Jacobo, el padre de la familia, tiene como objetivo ampliar el tamaño de su granja, tener más animales y convertirla en una atracción turística. A Jacobo se le presenta una gran oportunidad por la venta de la granja vecina, y emprende junto al resto de su familia la remodelación de la granja para convertirla en lo que siempre quiso, un lugar con constantes visitas de familias y grupos.

The Villalobos is a family of four who live on a farm in the outskirts of Costa Rica. Jacobo, the father of the family, aims to expand the size of his farm, have more animals and turn it into a tourist attraction. Jacobo is presented with a great opportunity for the sale of the neighboring farm, and undertakes with the rest of his family the remodeling of the farm to make it what he always wanted, a place with constant visits from families and groups.

GRANJA LOS VILLALOBOS

Los Villalobos, una familia de cuatro **integrantes**, el señor Jacobo, la señora María y sus dos hijos Luciano y Sara viven en una **granja** ubicada en las **afueras** de Costa Rica.

Jacobo quien **hereda** la granja de su padre, siempre tuvo el sueño de hacer de ella una **atracción turística** y siempre que podía comprar más **hectáreas** lo hacía para ampliar su variedad de animales.

1. **Integrantes:** Members
2. **Granja**: Farm
3. **Afueras**: Outskirts
4. **Hereda**: Inherit
5. **Atracción turística**: Tourist attraction
6. **Hectáreas**: Hectares

Su hijo Luciano quien también ama a los animales como su padre, siempre ha querido tener un **espacio** en la granja especialmente para sus animales favoritos, que son las **aves**.

Luciano tiene una pequeña colección. Tiene una pareja de aves **quetzal**, un pájaro campana y una **lapa roja**. Les tiene mucho aprecio ya que los heredó de su abuelo.

Una mañana **nublada** la granja está muy tranquila y los animales descansan un tanto **perezosos** debido al **clima** tan fresco que había. No es una mañana **soleada** como **solía** ser. A lo lejos, se acerca el vecino.

7. **Espacio**: Space
8. **Aves:** Birds
9. **Quetzal:** A type of bird
10. **Lapa roja:** Scarlet macaw
11. **Nublada:** Cloudy
12. **Perezosos:** Lazy
13. **Clima**: Weather
14. **Soleada**: Sunny
15. **Solía:** Used to

Jacobo, saludando al **vecino**, le hace señas para que este se acerque a la casa y disfrute de un rico chocolate caliente.

—Hola vecino, ¿qué lo trae por aquí? —pregunta Jacobo.

El vecino responde:

—Solo paso a **saludar** y quiero comentarle un par de cosas, o mejor dicho, quiero proponerle un **negocio** —dijo el vecino.

16. **Vecino:** Neighbour
17. **Saludar**: To greet
18. **Negocio:** Deal

—A ver coménteme ese negocio del que habla —responde Luciano mientras sirve dos tazas de chocolate caliente.

—Lo que pasa es que mi **esposa** quiere **mudarse** a la ciudad y poder estar más **pendiente** del negocio que tenemos allá, entonces estoy pensando en **vender** mi granja —dice el vecino.

Jacobo se fue en pensamiento mientras su vecino seguía hablando. Solamente se **imaginaba** todo lo que iba a hacer si compraba esa granja.

19. **Esposa**: Wife
20. **Mudarse**: To move out
21. **Pendiente:** Attentive
22. **Vender**: To sell
23. **Imaginaba**: Imagined

—¡Jacobo! ¿Me escuchaste todo lo que dije? —pregunta el vecino **exaltado.**

—Sí disculpa, es que me **agrada** mucho la idea y solo me estaba imaginando todos los **planes** que tengo para esas **jugosas** siete hectáreas que tienes —dice Jacobo.

—Perfecto, mañana vendré con mi **abogado** para que podamos hacer los papeles y llevar todo de forma **legal** —dice el vecino.

24. **Exaltado:** Overexcited
25. **Me agrada:** I like
26. **Planes**: Plans
27. **Jugosas:** jucy
28. **Abogado**: Attorney
29. **Legal:** Legal

Se despiden ambos vecinos y Jacobo llama a sus hijos y a su esposa para contarles lo que le acaba de decir el vecino y todos los planes que tiene.

—Podemos ampliar nuestro corral, nuestro **establo** y podemos tener una **jaula** grande para poder **albergar** tus aves, Luciano —comenta muy emocionado Jacobo.

Llega el día siguiente, esta vez sí era una mañana soleada como la mayoría, pero a Jacobo eso no le importó y desde horas de la mañana ya estaba sentado en el **frente** de su casa esperando a su vecino.

—¡Vecino, vecino! —Escucha Jacobo a lo lejos, a lo que se asoma y ve a su vecino acercarse junto a un hombre con un **traje negro** y **sosteniendo** un **maletín** negro.

30. **Establo**: Barn
31. **Jaula**: Cage
32. **Albergar**: To harbor
33. **Frente**: Front
34. **Asoma: looks out**
35. **Traje negro**: Black suit
36. **Sosteniendo:** Holding
37. **Maletin**: Briefcase

—Buenos días, Jacobo, te presento a mi abogado que siempre me ha acompañado en todos mis negocios. Ya le comenté que quiero vender mi granja y él ha venido a hacerlo legal

—dice el vecino.

—Perfecto, vamos a **concretar** esto —dice Jacobo.

Pasaron dos horas **platicando** y **firmando** los papeles de su nueva **adquisición**. Finalmente, el vecino se despide con ojos llorosos debido a que acaba de vender su granja.

Pasaron dos meses durante los cuales Jacobo había dedicado tiempo para ampliar su granja, colocar nuevas **jaulas** y dividir por **zonas** los distintos animales que ya tenía y los nuevos que había comprado.

38. Concretar: To finalize

39. Platicando: Talking

40. Firmando: Signing

41. Adquisición: Acquisition

42. Jaulas: Cages

43. Zonas: Areas

Las áreas para las **vacas**, los **cerdos**, los **caballos** y hasta pequeños **ponis** estaban todos con sus respectivas **cercas**, áreas para comer y para la **recreación** de los animales.

Uno de los más contentos por la nueva granja y por la nueva ampliación era su hijo Luciano, ya que finalmente tenía su espacio para sus aves.

44. Vacas: Cows

45. Cerdos: Pigs

46. Caballos: Horses

47. Ponis: Ponies

48. Cercas: Fences

49. Recreación: Recreation

Finalizada la ampliación de la granja, se reúnen en familia para la **planificación** de las áreas de atracción turística, desde una pequeña **granja de contacto** para los visitantes más pequeños hasta largas **caminatas** a caballo.

En la reunión todos opinan:

—La granja de contacto tendrá animales pequeños como cerdos, **ovejas** y ponis para que los niños puedan jugar y alimentarlos —opina Sara.

—Buena idea, y las **cabalgatas** a caballo serán por el **sendero** norte que llegarán a la **colina** para ver el **atardecer** —dice Jacobo.

50. Planificación: Planning

51. Granja de contacto: Petting farm

52. Caminatas: Walks

53. Ovejas: Sheep

54. Cabalgatas: Horseback riding

55. Sendero: Path

56. Colina: Hill

57. Atardecer: Sunset

—Me parece muy **romántico** la idea de las cabalgatas, tienen que ser exclusivas para las **parejas** que nos visiten —acota la señora María.

—Estaba pensando que una **actividad familiar** sería que todos puedan **ordeñar** una vaca y que vieran el proceso de cómo se hace la leche —**agrega** Luciano—. Al finalizar su tarde en la granja se podrán tomar una foto de recuerdo con mis bellas aves.

124

58. **Romántico**: Romantic

59. **Parejas**: Couples

60. **Actividad familiar:** Family activity

61. **Ordeñar**: To milk

62. **Agrega:** Adds

Al terminar la reunión familiar, planifican cuándo será la gran **apertura** de la granja para el público, comienzan todos los **preparativos** y realizan un gran cartel que anuncia el día de apertura.

Llegado el día de apertura, muchas personas emocionadas por conocer la hermosa granja de los Villalobos, se reúnen en la gran puerta de **tablas de madera** esperando la hora de entrada.

Los Villalobos, un poco **angustiados** por todos los detalles para que la gran **inauguración** al público salga bien, se dividen las **tareas** del día y Jacobo dice:

—Sofía, tú te vas a encargar de los niños en la granja de contacto, **asegúrate** que los alimenten y jueguen con ellos. María, tú organiza la cabalgata a caballo de las parejas y Luciano, prepara la **cámara** para las fotos con tus aves.

63. **Apertura**: Opening

64. **Preparativos**: Preparations

65. **Tablas de madera**: Wooden boards

66. **Angustiados:** Preoccupied

67. **Inauguración**: Opening

68. **Tareas:** Tasks

69. **Asegúrate:** You make sure

70. **Cámara**: Camera

Luciano pregunta:

—¿Y tú papá, qué harás?

—Yo prepararé a las vacas con sus respectivos **becerros** y **cubetas** para que las familias las puedan ordeñar, previo a un pequeño **curso** de cómo hacerlo. —responde Jacobo.

Llega la hora de abrir las puertas y entre **globos** y música los visitantes entran a la hermosa granja de los Villalobos. **Asombrados** por lo que ven, comentan:

—¡Qué hermosa es!, no puedo creer que exista un lugar tan bello y familiar en Costa Rica —dice una mamá que visita la granja con sus dos pequeños hijos.

—Tenemos una granja de contacto donde sus pequeños hijos pueden estar con lindos animales, **darles de comer** y jugar con ellos —le dice Sofía a la mamá.

71. **Becerros**: Calves
72. **Cubetas**: Buckets
73. **Curso**: Course
74. **Globos**: Balloons
75. **Asombrados:** Amazed
76. **Darles de comer**: Feed them

Los niños saltan de la emoción y corren a donde se encuentra la granja de contacto.

Muy emocionados los niños exclaman:

—¡Mira, mamá, un bebé cerdito y una pequeña **oveja**!, les daré de comer con este biberón.

—Son muy lindos, **trátenlos** con **cuidado** y amor —le dice la mamá a sus hijos.

Al otro lado de la granja la señora María reúne a las parejas **asistentes** y les ofrece una romántica cabalgata a caballo hasta la colina, donde verán el hermoso atardecer y al finalizar degustarán unos ricos **aperitivos**.

Una pareja de **recién casados**, interesados en el paseo, comenta:

—Me parece interesante ese paseo, ¿podemos **escoger** los caballos? —pregunta el esposo.

77. **Oveja:** Sheep
78. **Trátenlos:** Treat them (instructions)
79. **Cuidado**: Care
80. **Asistentes:** Participating
81. **Aperitivos:** Appetizers
82. **Recién casados:** Just married
83. **Escoger**: To choose

—Claro que sí; vengan al establo y les muestro los caballos **ensillados** —responde María.

Al ir al establo, encuentran unos hermosos caballos **pura sangre** y María se los presenta:

—Este caballo negro es **Cometa**, es muy dócil y le encanta la **zanahoria**, este caballo blanco de aquí es **Copo de Nieve**, es muy **veloz** y le encanta que le **trencen** su cola.

84. **Ensillados:** Saddled
85. **Pura sangre:** Pure blood
86. **Cometa:** Comet or kite
87. **Zanahoria:** Carrot
88. **Copo de Nieve:** Snowflake
89. **Veloz:** Fast
90. **Trencen**: Braid

—¡Me gusta Copo de Nieve!, ese será mi caballo —dice la esposa entusiasmada.

—Entonces el mío será Cometa, me encantan los **caballos negros** —responde el esposo que visita la granja.

—Está bien, **móntense** en sus respectivos caballos que les espera una hermosa **puesta de sol** —dice María a la pareja de recién casados.

La pareja inicia la cabalgata por un hermoso sendero cubierto de un **césped** totalmente verde, con un clima **agradable** y escuchando los sonidos característicos de todos los animales que **habitan** en la granja.

91. **Caballos negros:** Black horses
92. **Móntense:** Mount (a horse)
93. **Puesta de sol:** Sunset
94. **Césped**: Grass
95. **Agradable:** Nice
96. **Habitan**: They inhabit (verb: habitar)

El señor Jacobo se reúne con las familias asistentes y les dicta una breve **charla** de como es el **proceso** de obtención de leche de vaca, y pregunta a los asistentes:

—¿Alguien quiere ordeñar una de estas hermosas **vacas mariposas**?

Y del grupo de asistentes, un padre y un hijo gritan emocionados:

—¡Nosotros, nosotros!

El señor Jacobo les pide que **se acerquen** a donde está la vaca junto a su pequeño becerro y dice que uno de los dos se siente en un **taburete de madera** muy bajo, que los ayudará a **alcanzar** las **ubres** de la vaca.

97. **Dicta:** Gives/Presents

98. **Charla**: Chat

99. **Proceso:** Process

100. **Vacas mariposas:** White cows with black spots

101.**Se acerquen:** They approach

102. **Taburete de madera**: Wooden stool

103. **Alcanzar:** To reach

104. **Ubres**: Udders

El padre de familia se sienta y coloca a su hijo en su **regazo**, toman como les había enseñado previamente Jacobo las ubres de la vaca y empiezan a ordeñarlas.

El niño muy entusiasmado le dice al papá:

—¡Papá, es leche como la que como con mi cereal!

Todas las familias asistentes se ríen y continúan observando el proceso de obtención de leche.

Mientras tanto, un grupo de **jóvenes** se encuentran con Luciano en el área de las jaulas de aves, y extasiados por los hermosos colores de cada **especie** de ave y por sus peculiares **cantos**, se toman fotos con cada una de ellas.

105. **Regazo:** Lap

106. **Mientras tanto:** Meanwhile

107. **Jóvenes:** Young boys

108. **Extasiados:** Captivated

109. **Especie**: Species

110.**Cantos:** Songs

—Quiero una foto con el ave en mi cabeza —dice un joven emocionado.

—¡Mi foto será alimentando al ave azul! —exclama otra joven del grupo.

Jacobo **complace** a todos los presentes y les **entrega** su foto como **recuerdo** de la visita a la granja.

Al finalizar el día de apertura de la granja, toda la familia Villalobos se reúne para la cena y concluyen, que la inauguración de la granja para el público ha sido todo un **éxito** y que lo harían cada **fin de semana** de sus vidas.

111. **Complace:** pleases
112. **Entrega:** gives
113. **Recuerdo**: Memory
114. **Éxito**: Success
115. **Fin de semana**: Weekend

GRANJA LOS VILLALOBOS
PREGUNTAS

1. **¿De quién heredó las aves Luciano?**
   a. De su padre
   b. De su abuelo
   c. De su hermana

2. **¿Qué actividad planeaban para los visitantes más pequeños?**
   a. Paseos a caballos
   b. Fotos con las aves
   c. Granja de contacto

3. **¿Quién organiza las cabalgatas para las parejas?**
   a. María
   b. Sofía
   c. Luciano

4. **¿Qué caballo escoge el esposo que visita la granja?**
   a. Copo de Nieve
   b. Cometa
   c. Lapa roja

5. **¿Cuándo harán más aperturas al público luego de la exitosa inauguración?**
   a. Todos los días
   b. Nunca
   c. Cada fin de semana

GRANJA LOS VILLALOBOS
SOLUCIONES

1. B

2. C

3. A

4. B

5. C

GRANJA LOS VILLALOBOS
VOCABULARIO

1. **Integrantes:** Members
2. **Granja**: Farm
3. **Afueras**: Outskirts
4. **Hereda**: Inherit
5. **Atracción turística**: Tourist attraction
6. **Hectáreas**: Hectares
7. **Espacio**: Space
8. **Aves:** Birds
9. **Quetzal:** A type of bird
10. **Lapa roja:** Scarlet macaw
11. **Nublada:** Cloudy
12. **Perezosos:** Lazy
13. **Clima**: Weather
14. **Soleada**: Sunny
15. **Solía:** Used to
16. **Vecino:** Neighbour
17. **Saludar**: To greet
18. **Negocio:** Deal
19. **Esposa**: Wife
20. **Mudarse**: To move out
21. **Pendiente:** Attentive
22. **Vender**: To sell
23. **Imaginaba**: Imagined
24. **Agrada:** pleases
25. **Planes**: Plans
26. **Abogado**: Attorney
27. **Legal:** Legal
28. **Establo**: Barn
29. **Jaula**: Cage
30. **Albergar**: To harbor
31. **Frente**: Front
32. **Traje negro**: Black suit
33. **Sosteniendo:** Holding
34. **Maletín**: Briefcase
35. **Concretar**: To finalize
36. **Platicando**: Talking
37. **Firmando**: Signing
38. **Adquisición:** Acquisition
39. **Jaulas**: Cages
40. **Zonas**: Areas
41. **Vacas:** Cows
42. **Cerdos:** Pigs
43. **Caballos**: Horses
44. **Ponis**: Ponies
45. **Cercas:** Fences
46. **Recreación:** Recreation
47. **Planificación:** Planning

48. **Granja de contacto**: Contact farm/Petting farm
49. **Caminatas**: Walks
50. **Ovejas:** Sheep
51. **Cabalgatas**: Horseback riding
52. **Sendero**: Path
53. **Colina**: Hill
54. **Atardecer:** Sunset
55. **Romántico**: Romantic
56. **Parejas**: Couples
57. **Actividad familiar:** Family activity
58. **Ordeñar**: To milk
59. **Agrega:** Adds
60. **Apertura**: Opening
61. **Preparativos**: Preparations
62. **Tablas de madera**: Wooden boards
63. **Angustiados:** Preoccupied
64. **Inauguración**: Opening
65. **Tareas:** Tasks
66. **Asegúrate:** You make sure
67. **Cámara**: Camera
68. **Becerros**: Calves
69. **Cubetas**: Buckets
70. **Curso**: Course
71. **Globos**: Balloons
72. **Asombrados:** Amazed
73. **Darles de comer**: Feed them
74. **Trátenlos:** Treat them (instructions)
75. **Cuidado**: Care
76. **Aperitivos:** Appetizers
77. **Recién casados:** Just married
78. **Escoger**: To choose
79. **Ensillados:** Saddled
80. **Pura sangre:** Pure blood
81. **Cometa:** Comet or kite
82. **Zanahoria:** Carrot
83. **Copo de Nieve:** Snowflake
84. **Veloz:** Fast
85. **Trencen**: Braid
86. **Caballos negros:** Black horses
87. **Móntense:** Mount (a horse)
88. **Puesta de sol:** Sunset
89. **Césped**: Grass
90. **Agradable:** Nice
91. **Habitan**: They inhabit (Verb: habitar)
92. **Charla**: Chat

93. **Proceso:** Process
94. **Vacas mariposas:** White cows with black spots
95. **Taburete de madera**: Wooden stool
96. **Alcanzar:** To reach
97. **Ubres**: Udders
98. **Regazo:** Lap
99. **Mientras tanto:** Meanwhile
100. **Jóvenes:** Young boys
101. **Especie**: Species
102. **Cantos:** Songs
103. **Complace:** Pleases
104. **Entrega:** Gives
105. **Recuerdo**: Memory
106. **Éxito**: Success
107. **Fin de semana**: Weekend

UN EMPRENDEDOR NATO
RESUMEN

José es un chico emprendedor que siempre le ha preocupado la forma en que actualmente vive con su familia y decide tomar la decisión de cambiar su vida y la de su familia por completo. Decide irse a otro país donde encuentra un trabajo totalmente inesperado que va a ser el primer escalón para poder cumplir su máximo sueño.

José is an entrepreneur guy who has always worried about the way he currently lives with his family and decides to make the decision to change his and his family's lives completely. He decides to go to another country where he finds a totally unexpected job that will be the first step in order to fulfill his maximum dream

UN EMPRENDEDOR NATO

José es un chico de **bajo nivel socioeconómico proveniente** del país Paraguay, quien **decide emprender** una nueva **aventura** y **dirigirse** a otro país para poder tener una mejor **calidad** de vida y así poder ayudar a su familia que tanto lo necesita.

1. **Bajo nivel socioeconómico:** Low socioeconomic status
2. **Proveniente:** Coming
3. **Decide:** Decides
4. **Emprender:** To undertake
5. **Aventura:** Adventure
6. **Dirigirse:** Heads towards

7. **Calidad:** Quality

Una tarde toma la decisión de hacer las maletas y emprender su aventura al día siguiente. **Sorprendiendo** a sus familiares, decide darles la gran **noticia**.

—Familia, tengo una noticia muy importante que darles. He decidido **marcharme** a otro país para que todos podamos tener la vida que nos merecemos —dice José a sus familiares.

8. **Sorprendiendo:** Surprising
9. **Noticia:** News
10. **Marcharme:** Leaving

Sorprendidos todos por la **impactante** noticia, la mamá de José, Pierina, con **lágrimas** de **confusión** y **alegría** en sus **ojos**, responde:

—¡Qué alegría, hijo! Sé que estás **destinado** para grandes cosas y sabemos que te irá excelente porque siempre fuiste un chico **emprendedor** y que sabe lo que quiere.

11. **Impactante:** Shocking
12. **Lágrimas:** Tears
13. **Confusión:** Confusion
14. **Alegría:** Joy
15. **Ojos:** Eyes
16. **Destinado:** Destined
17. **Emprendedor:** Entrepreneur

Al día siguiente, José se prepara para **enfrentar** lo que será sin lugar a **dudas** su mayor aventura.

Con una gran maleta a la **derecha** de su **cuerpo**, un bolso en su **espalda**, ambas cosas **llenas** de **esperanzas,** y una **sensación** increíble de **plenitud** de que todo en su vida está por mejorar, llega al **aeropuerto** donde se monta en un **avión**, rumbo a Panamá.

18. **Enfrentar:** To face or confront
19. **Dudas:** Doubts
20. **Derecha:** Right
21. **Cuerpo:** Body
22. **Espalda:** Back
23. **Llenas:** Full
24. **Esperanzas:** Hopes
25. **Sensación:** Sensation
26. **Plenitud:** Fullness
27. **Aeropuerto:** Airport
28. **Avión:** Airplane
29. **Rumbo:** Bound for

Al llegar al Aeropuerto Internacional de Tocumen, **ubicado** en la ciudad de Panamá, se dispone a tomar un bus en la **estación** más cercana del aeropuerto y así dirigirse al centro para poder **alquilar** una **habitación** en un **hostal**.

Está sorprendido por la gran ciudad de Panamá y ver a toda la gente caminando, **luciendo** felicidad **plena**, cosa que en su **barrio** nunca pudo apreciar porque siempre está ocupado **trabajando**.

30. **Ubicado:** Located
31. **Estación:** Station
32. **Alquilar:** To rent

33. **Habitación:** Room
34. **Hostal:** Hostel
35. **Luciendo:** Appearing
36. **Plena:** Complete/Full
37. **Barrio:** Neighborhood
38. **Trabajando:** Working

Llega al centro, donde pudo **detectar** a lo lejos un hostal con un **cartel** luminoso que decía en grande «**habitaciones disponibles**», decide dirigirse a esa **dirección** y **averiguar**.

Cuando entra al hostal, se dirige a la persona **detrás** del **mostrador**, quien podía verse a través del mismo con un poco de dificultad debido a su poca **estatura**.

39. **Detectar:** To detect
40. **Cartel:** Sign
41. **Habitaciones disponibles:** Rooms available
42. **Dirección:** Address
43. **Averiguar:** Find out
44. **Detrás:** Behind
45. **Mostrador:** Counter
46. **Estatura:** Height

—Buenas tardes, bienvenido al hostal El Valle, ¿en qué puedo ayudarlo? — pregunta la persona detrás del mostrador con un **acento** que no es de la **localidad**.

—Buenas tardes, tu acento me **resulta** muy familiar, ¿eres de nacionalidad panameña?

—pregunta José con un **tono** de **curiosidad**.

47. **Acento:** Accent

48. **Localidad:** Location

49. **Resulta:** Appears

50. **Tono:** Tone

51. **Curiosidad:** Curiosity

—No, **de hecho** soy paraguayo, me mudé primero a Colombia y luego a Panamá hace dos años. Me llamo Antonio —responde la persona detrás del mostrador.

—Excelente, yo también soy de Paraguay, decidí venir a esta ciudad en busca de una mejor vida y poder ayudar a mi familia. Estoy seguro que me entenderás —dice José.

—Sí, lo mismo vine a hacer yo aquí y me ha resultado de **maravilla**. Espero poder ayudarte en todo lo que pueda. ¿Quisieras una habitación? —pregunta Antonio.

—Sí, por favor, ya necesito **moverme** en búsqueda de algún trabajo —dice José.

Antonio le da la habitación número cinco, ubicada en el **primer piso** del hostal en el **ala derecha.**

Luego de que José se acomodara en su nuevo cuarto, decide leer los **folletos** que había visto en la **recepción** del hostal, **motivo** por el cual decide bajar **rápidamente.**

52. **De hecho:** In fact

53. **Maravilla:** Wonder

54. **Moverme:** For me to get started

55. **Búsqueda:** A search

56. **Primer piso:** First floor

57. **Ala derecha:** Right wing

58. **Folletos:** Brochures

59. **Recepción:** Reception

60. **Motivo:** Reason

61. **Rápidamente:** Quickly

Encuentra un gran anuncio en el primer folleto que ve que le llama la atención, **debido a** su gran **tamaño** que dice «¿Tienes experiencia al **volante?** Buscamos **conductores** con ganas de **superarse** y **ascender** a la **cima**».

Emocionado por el folleto, decide rápidamente dirigirse a las oficinas de esa agencia de viajes **terrestres** que se ubicaba a **escasas** tres cuadras del hostal El Valle.

62. **Debido a:** Due to
63. **Tamaño:** Size
64. **Volante:** Steering Wheel
65. **Conductores:** Drivers
66. **Superarse:** To improve oneself
67. **Ascender:** To climb
68. **Cima:** Top
69. **Terrestres:** Terrestrial/Ground
70. **Escasas:** Mere/Barely

Al llegar, inmediatamente le dice el chico que atiende en el local:

—Por su cara de **entusiasmo me atrevería** a decir que viene por el anuncio del folleto y déjeme decirle que llegó en el momento más **indicado**.

—Sí, vine por el anuncio ya que estoy **interesado** en el trabajo —dice entusiasmado José.

—Perfecto, en este momento estamos **contratando** de forma **inmediata**, solo tiene que pasar por una rápida **entrevista** con nuestro **gerente** que se encuentra en su oficina. Pase por aquí, por favor —dice el chico.

71. **Entusiasmo:** Enthusiasm

72. **Me atrevería:** I would dare

73. **Indicado:** Indicated/Right

74. **Interesado:** Interested

75. **Contratando:** Hiring

76. **Inmediata:** Immediate

77. **Entrevista:** Interview

78. **Gerente:** Manager

El chico lleva a José a la oficina del gerente. Luego de tener una **minuciosa** entrevista de dos horas, finalmente el gerente le dice que puede comenzar a trabajar el día siguiente como conductor de un **gran bus azul** para hacer **viajes cortos** dentro de la misma ciudad.

José, emocionado, se dirige a su habitación para poder **descansar** y poder empezar a trabajar con su mejor **actitud**.

79. **Minuciosa:** Thorough
80. **Gran bus azul:** Great blue bus
81. **Viajes:** Travels/Trips
82. **Cortos:** Shorts
83. **Descansar:** Rest
84. **Actitud:** Attitude

Lo que más le gusta a José de su nuevo trabajo es que tiene la **posibilidad** de **ascender de cargo** e ir desde el conductor del bus, hasta dirigir alguna de las estaciones de bus de la empresa, hasta poder llegar a ser el presidente **de dicha** compañía.

Llega el día tan esperado y en el local ya lo estaban esperando para entregarle su **vestimenta** acorde a la empresa, que **constaba de** una camisa azul **manga larga** con el nombre de la empresa.

85. **Posibilidad:** Possibility
86. **Ascender de cargo:** Advance one's career
87. **De dicha:** Of said
88. **Vestimenta:** Clothing
89. **Constaba de:** Consisted of
90. **Manga larga:** Long sleeve

Le comentan que su primer viaje será para el pueblo Boquete, luego se le **asignarían** otros destinos más largos como para los pueblos de Pedasí y Portobelo.

Finalmente llega su primer viaje, emocionado le da la bienvenida a todos los **pasajeros** que van entrando al bus y los saluda desde el puesto del conductor.

—Bienvenidos a todos, mi nombre es José y soy su conductor para llevarlos a su destino, el maravilloso pueblo de Boquete. Son aproximadamente dos horas de viaje. Cualquier cosa no **duden** en preguntarme —informa José a sus pasajeros.

José, un poco nervioso ya que es su primer viaje y no conoce del todo la ciudad de Panamá, decide preguntarle a su **acompañante** Juan, quien estaría junto a él **supervisándolo** por si surge algún **inconveniente**.

91. **Asignaría:** Would assign (verb: asignar)
92. **Pasajeros:** Passengers
93. **Duden:** You all hesitate
94. **Acompañante:** Companion
95. **Supervisándolo:** Supervising (verb: supervisar)
96. **Inconveniente:** Problem

—¿Qué pasa José? Te noto un poco nervioso —dice Juan.

—Pues sí, la verdad es que estoy nervioso, tengo **miedo** de olvidar la **ruta** que me aprendí esta mañana cuando me estaba vistiendo —dice José con palabras entre cortadas.

—No te preocupes, José, se me había olvidado comentarte, aquí podemos usar el GPS que nos da la ruta exacta, la más corta y la que tiene **menos tráfico** —dice Juan entre **carcajadas** ya que José estaba nervioso y tenían la solución perfecta a su preocupación.

97. **Miedo:** Fear
98. **Ruta:** Route
99. **Menos tráfico:** Less trafic
100. **Carcajadas:** Laughter

Un pasajero se levanta del **asiento trasero** y se acerca a José para preguntarle lo siguiente:

—Hola, José, este autobús llega **directamente** al pueblo Boquete, ¿verdad?

—Sí, los llevaré directamente a la estación principal de allá, no se preocupe por eso —dice José en un tono **amable**.

—Siempre tomo este autobús, pero preguntaba porque es la primera vez que te veo —dice el pasajero.

101. **Asiento trasero:** Back seat
102. **Directamente:** Directly
103. **Amable:** Friendly

—Sí, es mi primer viaje pero no te preocupes por nada, aquí a mi lado tengo a Juan quien tiene dos años de experiencia y cualquier cosa él nos puede ayudar.

—Perfecto, ¿será que podemos bajarnos en la **estación de gasolina** para ir al baño? —pregunta el pasajero.

—Sí, claro. La próxima estación de gasolina se encuentra a doscientos **metros** en dirección noroeste —explica José.

Al llegar a la estación, Juan **le hace saber** a José que está haciendo un increíble trabajo y que le preguntó a los pasajeros mientras él estaba **concentrado** en el camino acerca de qué les parecía el nuevo conductor.

José estaba un poco nervioso acerca de lo que pensaban los pasajeros. Juan le dice que todos estaban muy contentos debido a la **amabilidad** que José había mostrado durante todo el viaje.

104. **Estación de gasolina:** Gas station
105. **Metros:** Meters
106. **Le hace saber:** Let him know
107. **Concentrado:** Concentrated
108. **Amabilidad:** Friendliness

Luego de quince minutos, vuelven de nuevo a la **carretera**. José toma el **audio parlante** del autobús y les comenta a los pasajeros.

—Queridos pasajeros, estamos a escasos treinta minutos de llegar a nuestro **destino**. Mi compañero Juan pasará por sus asientos para cobrar la **tarifa** de este autobús que son $1,20.

Luego de llegar a su destino, los pasajeros bajan del autobús, seguido de Juan y José que fueron los últimos en bajarse.

109. **Carretera:** Road

110. **Audio parlante:** Speaker

111. **Destino:** Destination

112. **Tarifa:** Rate

Mientras se montaban los siguientes pasajeros que se dirigían al punto de partida del viaje anterior, José recibe una **llamada.** Era el gerente para **felicitarlo** ya que Juan le había comentado como le había ido y los comentarios de los pasajeros.

Debido a esa llamada, José pasó todo el viaje de regreso con una **sonrisa** de **oreja** a oreja porque sabía que lo había hecho de forma excelente.

Pasaron dos años, donde José había ascendido desde conductor del autobús, luego a **supervisor** de conductor, hasta que finalmente el gerente le comenta que durante estos largos dos años se ha podido ganar su entera confianza. Decide proponerle ser su **mano derecha** y así dirigir sus empresas de la ciudad de panamá.

113. **Llamada:** Call

114. **Felicitarlo:** Congratulate (verb: felicitar)

115. **Sonrisa:** Smile

116. **Oreja:** Ear

117. **Supervisor:** Supervisor

118. **Mano derecha:** Right hand

José, emocionado por su nuevo ascenso, llama a su familia para darles tan increíble noticia. Les comenta que finalmente podrá ayudarlos como siempre ha querido y no darle solamente **remesas mensualmente** para poder vivir un poco mejor que antes.

Pasados tres meses en su nuevo puesto, José tuvo la oportunidad de comprar una casa con cuatro cuartos, tres baños, una cocina y un **gran patio trasero**.

Luego de un mes de mudarse, pudo hacer y **concretar** el **objetivo principal** de aquella aventura, que era llevar a su familia a vivir con él para que no tengan que pasar más necesidades en su vida y tener la vida que tanto se merecen todos.

119. **Remesas:** Remittances/Money
120. **Mensualmente:** Monthly
121. **Gran patio trasero:** Large backyard
122. **Concretar:** To fullfill
123. **Objetivo principal:** Main goal

UN EMPRENDEDOR NATO
PREGUNTAS

1. ¿Dónde vive actualmente José?

    a. Panamá

    b. Boquete

    c. Paraguay

2. ¿Qué nacionalidad tiene Antonio?

    a. Paraguaya

    b. Panameña

    c. Colombiana

3. ¿Qué es lo que más le gusta a José de su trabajo?

    a. Ser conductor del autobús

    b. La posibilidad de ascender en la compañía

    c. Ser gerente

4. ¿Cuál es el primer destino de José?

    a. Boquete

    b. Pedasí

    c. Portobelo

5. ¿Cuántos años pasaron para que José tuviera su máximo ascenso?

    a. Un año

    b. Tres años

    c. Dos años

UN EMPRENDEDOR NATO
SOLUCIONES

1. A

2. A

3. B

4. A

5. C

UN EMPRENDEDOR NATO
VOCABULARIO

1. **Bajo nivel socioeconómico:** Low socioeconomic status
2. **Proveniente:** Coming
3. **Decide:** Decides
4. **Emprender:** To undertake
5. **Aventura:** Adventure
6. **Dirigirse:** Heads towards
7. **Calidad:** Quality
8. **Sorprendiendo:** Surprising
9. **Noticia:** News
10. **Marcharme:** Leaving
11. **Impactante:** Shocking
12. **Lágrimas:** Tears
13. **Confusión:** Confusion
14. **Alegría:** Joy
15. **Ojos:** Eyes
16. **Destinado:** Destined
17. **Emprendedor:** Entrepreneur
18. **Enfrentar:** To face or confront
19. **Dudas:** Doubts
20. **Derecha:** Right
21. **Cuerpo:** Body
22. **Espalda:** Back
23. **Llenas:** Full
24. **Esperanzas:** Hopes
25. **Sensación:** Sensation
26. **Plenitud:** Fullness
27. **Aeropuerto:** Airport
28. **Avión:** Airplane
29. **Ubicado:** Located
30. **Estación:** Station
31. **Alquilar:** To rent
32. **Habitación:** Room
33. **Hostal:** Hostel
34. **Felicidad:** Happiness
35. **Barrio:** Neighborhood
36. **Trabajando:** Working
37. **Detectar:** To detect
38. **Cartel:** Sign
39. **Habitaciones disponibles:** Rooms available
40. **Dirección:** Address
41. **Averiguar:** To find out
42. **Detrás:** Behind
43. **Mostrador:** Counter
44. **Estatura:** Height
45. **Acento:** Accent

46. **Localidad:** Location
47. **Resulta:** Appears
48. **Tono:** Tone
49. **Curiosidad:** Curiosity
50. **De hecho:** In fact
51. **Maravilla:** Wonder
52. **Moverme:** For me to get started
53. **Búsqueda:** A search
54. **Primer piso:** First floor
55. **Ala derecha:** Right wing
56. **Folletos:** Brochures
57. **Recepción:** Reception
58. **Motivo:** Reason
59. **Rápidamente:** Quickly
60. **Debido a:** Due to
61. **Tamaño:** Size
62. **Volante:** Steering Wheel
63. **Conductores:** Drivers
64. **Superarse:** To improve oneself
65. **Ascender:** To climb
66. **Cima:** Top
67. **Terrestres:** Terrestrial/Ground
68. **Escasas:** Mere/Barely
69. **Entusiasmo:** Enthusiasm
70. **Me atrevería:** I would dare
71. **Indicado:** Indicated
72. **Interesado:** Interested
73. **Contratando:** Hiring
74. **Inmediata:** Immediate
75. **Entrevista:** Interview
76. **Gerente:** Manager
77. **Minuciosa:** Thorough
78. **Gran bus azul:** Great blue bus
79. **Viajes:** Travels/Trips
80. **Cortos:** Shorts
81. **Descansar:** To rest
82. **Actitud:** Attitude
83. **Posibilidad:** Possibility
84. **Ascender de cargo:** Advance one's career
85. **De dicha:** Of said
86. **Vestimenta:** Clothing
87. **Manga larga:** Long sleeve
88. **Asignaría:** Would assign (verb: asignar)
89. **Pasajeros:** Passengers
90. **Duden:** You all hesitate
91. **Acompañante:** Companion

92. **Supervisándolo:** Supervising
93. **Inconveniente:** Problem
94. **Miedo:** Fear
95. **Ruta:** Route
96. **Menos tráfico:** Less trafic
97. **Carcajadas:** Laughter
98. **Asiento trasero:** Back seat
99. **Directamente:** Directly
100. **Amable:** Friendly
101. **Estación de gasolina:** Gas station
102. **Metros:** Meters
103. **Le hace saber:** Let him know
104. **Concentrado:** Concentrated
105. **Amabilidad:** Friendliness
106. **Carretera:** Road
107. **Audio parlante:** Speaker
108. **Destino:** Destination
109. **Tarifa:** Rate
110. **Llamada:** Call
111. **Felicitarlo:** Congratulate (verb: felicitar)
112. **Sonrisa:** Smile
113. **Oreja:** Ear
114. **Supervisor:** Supervisor
115. **Mano derecha:** Right hand
116. **Remesas:** Remittances/Money
117. **Mensualmente:** Monthly
118. **Gran patio trasero:** Large backyard
119. **Concretar:** To fullfill
120. **Objetivo principal:** Main goal

HOSPITAL MARIO GARCÍA
RESUMEN

Mario, es un médico egresado de la Universidad del Zulia, en Venezuela. Desde los inicios de su carrera le ha gustado ayudar a los más necesitados, por lo que decide, luego de graduarse, trabajar en una zona rural. Le ofrecen un trabajo en la zona rural de un estado vecino llamado Pueblo Nuevo, el cual acepta. Luego de mucho tiempo ejerciendo su profesión en el pueblo, Mario se convierte en uno de los médicos favoritos de los habitantes y le agradecen inaugurando un hospital en su nombre.

Mario is a doctor graduated from the University of Zulia, in Venezuela. Since the beginning of his career, he decided to help the needy, which is why he decided to work in a rural area after his graduation. He gets a job offer in the rural area of a neighboring state called Pueblo Nuevo, which he accepts. After practicing his profession for a long time in the town, Mario becomes one of the favorite doctors of the people, and they thank him by opening a hospital in his name.

HOSPITAL MARIO GARCÍA

Mario García es un **médico cirujano egresado** de la ilustre Universidad del Zulia, en la **promoción** del año 2015, ubicada en la ciudad de Maracaibo, en el estado Zulia, Venezuela.

Siempre le ha gustado ayudar a las personas, motivo por el cual decide ir a un lugar rural para ayudar a aquellos que son **necesitados** y de **escasos recursos**.

1. **Médico**: Doctor

2. **Cirujano:** Surgeon
3. **Egresado:** A graduate
4. **Promoción:** Class
5. **Necesitados**: People in need
6. **Escasos recursos:** Scarce resources

Pocos meses después de su **graduación** recibe una llamada para un **puesto de trabajo** como médico del pueblo llamado Pueblo nuevo, ubicado en un estado cercano al de su nacimiento.

7. **Graduación:** Graduation
8. **Puesto de trabajo**: Job

Este es un pueblo pequeño de **apenas** cinco mil **habitantes** que está caracterizado por tener personas **amables**, **cariñosas** y muy **acogedoras**, siempre dispuestas a ayudar a quienes lo necesitan.

9. **Apenas**: Barely
10. **Habitantes:** Inhabitants
11. **Amables:** Friendly
12. **Cariñosas:** Affectionate
13. **Acogedoras:** Welcoming

El día anterior a su viaje, **agarra** la primera maleta que ve en su armario, coloca cinco **uniformes médicos**, su impecable **bata** blanca, el **estetoscopio**, el equipo de **otorrinolaringología**, el **martillo** para los **reflejos**, el **tensiómetro** y finalmente un **glucómetro**, revisando una y otra vez para no olvidar nada.

14. **Agarra:** Grabs
15. **Uniformes médicos:** Medical uniforms
16. **Bata:** Lab coat
17. **Estetoscopio:** Stethoscope
18. **Otorrinolaringología:** Otorhinolaryngology
19. **Martillo**: Hammer
20. **Reflejos:** Reflexes
21. **Tensiómetro**: Blood pressure cuff
22. **Glucómetro:** Glucometer

Una vez que llega al pueblo, es recibido por las personas que trabajan en el hospital, quienes le dan la **bienvenida**.

Luego de un almuerzo, con la comida típica del pueblo, le explican su **horario**, diciéndole cuáles son los días de **consulta** y los días de **visita domiciliaria**, para aquellas personas que no pueden **trasladarse** al hospital por alguna **discapacidad**.

23. **Bienvenida:** Welcome
24. **Horario:** Schedule
25. **Consulta:** Consultation
26. **Visita domiciliaria:** Home visit
27. **Trasladarse:** To move locations
28. **Discapacidad:** Disability

Emocionado por su primer día de consulta, se pone su uniforme favorito, el de color verde y encima de eso su **bata blanca**.

Pocos minutos después de su llegada al **consultorio**, el primer paciente toca a su puerta.

29. **Bata blanca:** White coat

30. **Consultorio:** Doctor's office

—Adelante —dice Mario.

—Buenos días, doctor, ¿cómo le va? —dice el primer paciente, un **albañil** del pueblo.

—Buenos días. ¿Cuál es su nombre? —pregunta Mario.

—Mi nombre es Agustín —responde el paciente.

—Tome asiento, señor Agustín, ¿en qué puedo ayudarle hoy? —pregunta Mario.

—Bueno doctor, resulta que desde hace cuatro días estoy presentando **dolor muscular**, **aumento** de la **temperatura corporal** y **escalofríos** y para el día de hoy me comenzaron a doler los **ojos** —refiere el paciente con preocupación.

31. **Albañil**: Construction worker
32. **Dolor muscular:** Muscle pain
33. **Aumento**: Increase
34. **Temperatura corporal:** Body temperature
35. **Escalofríos**: Shaking chills
36. **Ojos:** Eyes

Mario responde y pregunta:

—Ya veo, **por casualidad** ¿se hizo usted alguna **prueba de laboratorio?**

—Sí, doctor, yo me hice un **examen de sangre por mi cuenta** —dice el paciente y le entrega un papel con los **resultados**.

—**Puedo ver** que tiene una **infección**. Los resultados del examen y todos sus **síntomas** hablan de un **proceso viral** – dice Mario.

37. **Por casualidad**: By chance

38. **Prueba**: Test/exam

39. **Examin de Sangre**: Blood test/hematology

40. **Por mi cuenta:** On my own

41. **Resultados:** Results

42. **Puedo Ver:** I can see

43. **Infección:** Infection

44. **Síntomas:** Symptoms

45. **Proceso viral:** Viral process

—**O sea que**... ¿no es nada grave? —pregunta el paciente con incertidumbre.

—No, no es para nada grave pero tiene que **vigilar** si en el **transcurso** de esta semana presenta **dolor abdominal** o algún otro **síntoma**, por los momentos puede tomar cualquier **antigripal** y listo —dice Mario.

—Perfecto doctor, muchas gracias. Nos vemos la semana que viene para un nuevo **chequeo**, hasta luego —le dice el paciente muy agradecido.

—No se preocupe amigo, me hace el favor y me llama al **siguiente** paciente —dice Mario.

46. **O sea que**: In other words

47. **Vigilar**: To look out

48. **Transcurso:** Passing (of time)

49. **Dolor abdominal:** Abdominal pain

50. **Síntoma:** Symptom

51. **Antigripal:** Anti-flu

52. **Chequeo:** Check

53. **Siguiente**: Following

El paciente, muy conforme con la atención del doctor García, sale del consultorio con una gran sonrisa y se dispone a llamar al siguiente paciente.

En eso, entra una joven de veinticinco años **embarazada**, junto con su esposo.

—Muy buenos días, ¿cómo están? ¿Qué los trae por aquí hoy? —dice Mario con su característica sonrisa.

Responde la paciente:

—Doctor García, hoy vengo para mi consulta **prenatal**. Quisiera saber cómo va mi embarazo.

Mario le revisa los exámenes **pertinentes** como el **ecograma**, el **examen de orina**, calcula la **edad gestacional** a través del primer ecograma, la cual corresponde con su fecha de última regla.

54. **Embarazada:** Pregnant
55. **Prenatal:** Prenatal
56. **Pertinentes:** Pertinent
57. **Ecograma:** Ultrasound
58. **Examen de orina:** Urine test
59. **Edad gestacional**: Gestational age

Y le dice a la paciente:

—Hasta el momento su embarazo va en perfecta **evolución**, no tiene ningún tipo de **infección urinaria** y su fecha probable de **parto** es en aproximadamente tres meses. Pase a la **camilla** para que la **examine**.

60. **Evolución:** Evolution/Progress
61. **Infección urinaria**: Urinary infection
62. **Parto**: Birth

63. **Camilla:** Stretcher

64. **Examine:** Examine

La paciente se **dispone** a **acostarse** en la camilla, y con un poco de pena, ya que era la primera vez que asiste a la consulta del doctor, le pregunta:

—¿Tengo que colocarme esta bata que es transparente?

Mario como todo un profesional respetuoso le responde:

—Tranquila, solo veremos cómo está **creciendo** su **barriga** y escuchar los **latidos** de su **bebé**, para eso no es necesario que se coloque esta bata.

65. **Dispone**: Prepares

66. **Acostarse**: To lie down

67. **Creciendo**: Growing

68. **Barriga**: Belly

69. **Latidos**: Beats

70. **Bebé:** Baby

Luego de terminar con el **examen físico** de **rutina**, escuchar los fuertes latidos del bebé de la paciente, el doctor García le dice:

—Tal y como le dije anteriormente, todo está muy bien, la felicito, ha sacado una calificación perfecta en este **chequeo**, pero no se olvide que tiene que venir a consulta el mes siguiente para ver si todo sigue igual.

—Gracias, doctor, nos vemos el mes que viene, que tenga un feliz día y bienvenido al pueblo —le dice la paciente **satisfecha** con su consulta.

71. **Examen físico:** Physical exam

72. **Rutina:** Routine

73. **Chequeo:** Check

74. **Satisfecha:** Satisfied

Luego de ver aproximadamente a quince pacientes más, Mario se dirige a su casa para **descansar** del largo día que ha tenido.

De camino a su casa, pasa por la plaza principal del pueblo, donde todos los que ahí se encuentran comentan en voz baja y entre ellos, que él es el médico nuevo del pueblo y que según comentan era muy agradable y asertivo en sus **diagnósticos**.

75. **Descansar**: Rest

76. **Diagnósticos:** Diagnostics

Mario tratando de escuchar lo que dicen sus nuevos vecinos, se sienta en una banca y una vez ahí sentado, se le acerca un **señor mayor** y le pregunta:

—¿Es usted el nuevo médico del pueblo?

—Sí, es mi primer día de trabajo en el pueblo. ¿Lo puedo ayudar en algo? —pregunta Mario al **anciano** del pueblo.

—¡Qué bien! Un placer conocerle doctor. Hoy no lo voy a molestar, se nota algo **cansado**, mañana a primera hora estaré en la puerta de su consultorio para corroborar todo lo bueno que han comentado de usted —le dice el agradable anciano al doctor.

—Lo atenderé con mucho gusto, y espero cumplir sus **expectativas** —responde Mario.

77. **Señor mayor**: Old man

78. **Anciano**: Old man

79. **Cansado:** Tired

80. **Expectativas:** Expectations

Llega a su casa, se da una larga **ducha** y luego se duerme. Cuando menos lo espera, suena la alarma de su **despertador** y tiene que alistarse para comenzar un nuevo día.

Al entrar al hospital, todos los empleados y **enfermeras** lo saludan muy alegremente. Al estar cerca de la puerta de su consultorio, nota que el anciano de la plaza no está esperándolo.

Muy preocupado pregunta por el señor, y se da cuenta que es muy conocido en el pueblo. Pide su dirección y se dirige rápidamente hasta su casa para ver qué había pasado.

81. **Ducha:** Shower
82. **Despertador:** Alarm clock
83. **Enfermeras:** Nurses

Al llegar a la casa del anciano, Mario toca la puerta y por la puerta principal sale el anciano, el cual se notaba un poco cansado.

–¿Cómo está, señor?, lo estaba esperando en mi consultorio y al ver que no llegó quise venir a **atenderlo** en la **comodidad** de su casa —dice el Dr. García.

—No me siento muy bien, no me pude levantar de la cama más temprano y por eso no pude ir al hospital —responde el anciano.

Al pasar a la casa del anciano, el Doctor Mario se sienta con él en la sala y saca sus **instrumentos** de trabajo de su maletín para chequear al señor.

84. **Atenderlo:** Help him
85. **Comodidad:** Comfort
86. **Instrumentos:** Instruments

—¿Qué siente? —pregunta Mario.

—Me ha costado **respirar** últimamente, he tenido **fiebre** y mucha **tos** —responde el anciano con dificultad.

Mario toma su estetoscopio y lo coloca en el pecho del anciano para **auscultar** sus **pulmones**, escucha por el estetoscopio que tiene los **signos** de neumonía y le indica ciertos exámenes de **laboratorio** para asegurar su diagnóstico. Y le dice:

87. **Respirar**: To breathe
88. **Fiebre**: Fever
89. **Tos:** Cough
90. **Auscultar:** To listen to (medical examination)
91. **Pulmones:** Lungs
92. **Signos**: Signs
93. **Laboratorio:** Laboratory

—Tiene usted **neumonía**, le indicaré en una **receta** los **antibióticos** que tiene que tomar, para así mejorar su salud y volverlo a ver por la plaza en unos días. Mientras tanto tiene que seguir el tratamiento al pie de la letra y tener mucho **reposo**.

—¿Esta **enfermedad** es delicada para mi edad? —pregunta el anciano preocupado.

94. **Neumonía:** Pneumonia
95. **Receta**: Prescription
96. **Antibióticos:** Antibiotics
97. **Reposo:** Rest
98. **Enfermedad:** Disease

A lo que responde el Dr. García:

—Sí, lo es, pero si sigue el **tratamiento al pie de la letra**, será como una **gripe** cualquiera. Además, lo estaré visitando a **diario** para ver su evolución, no lo perderé de vista —responde Mario en tono **jocoso** para **disminuir** la preocupación de su paciente.

Pasan los días y Mario ha visitado al anciano cada vez que puede después de sus consultas, sigue su evolución y al cabo de unas semanas, el anciano mejora completamente.

99. **Tratamiento**: Treatment
100. **Al pie de la letra:** To the letter
101. **Gripe**: Flu
102. **Diario:** Daily
103. **Jocoso:** Humorous
104. **Disminuir:** To reduce

El señor mayor, muy agradecido por su atención y por su curación lo invita a almorzar a su casa cada vez que pueda y le dice:

—Has sido el mejor médico que ha pasado por este pueblo, desde tus diagnósticos asertivos hasta la sonrisa **sanadora** que tienes, para mí eres como un hijo.

—Muchas gracias por sus palabras. Desde el primer día de mi **carrera** este fue mi **propósito** y en este pueblo me encanta hacerlo, son personas muy cordiales que nunca voy a dejar de agradecerles —dice Mario **apenado** por las palabras del anciano.

105. **Sanadora:** Healing
106. **Carrera**: Career
107. **Propósito:** Intention
108. **Apenado:** Embarrassed/Saddened

Pasan los años y Mario se queda ejerciendo su **profesión** en Pueblo Nuevo. Los **pueblerinos** muy agradecidos con la labor del Dr. García siempre hacen **festejos** de agradecimientos en su nombre, hasta que un día es **remunerado** con algo muy importante, la **inauguración** de un pequeño hospital con su nombre.

El día de la esperada inauguración, Mario no puede creer lo que sus ojos ven, un gran **cartel** que dice «Hospital Dr. Mario García».

109. **Profesión:** Profession
110. **Pueblerinos**: Villagers
111. **Festejos**: Celebrations
112. **Remunerado:** Paid
113. **Inaguración:** Opening
114. **Cartel**: Sign

HOSPITAL MARIO GARCIA
PREGUNTAS

1. **¿Dónde decide ir Mario para ayudar a los más necesitados?**
   a. A la ciudad
   b. A una zona rural
   c. A otro país

2. **¿De qué color es su uniforme favorito?**
   a. Blanco
   b. Negro
   c. Verde

3. **¿Cuál fue el primer paciente de Mario?**
   a. El albañil del pueblo
   b. La joven embarazada
   c. El anciano

4. **¿Qué enfermedad le diagnostica el Doctor García al anciano?**
   a. Infección urinaria
   b. Virus
   c. Neumonía

5. **¿Cuál es la remuneración importante que recibe Mario por sus servicios?**
   a. Un gran almuerzo
   b. Una gran fiesta
   c. Un pequeño hospital con su nombre

HOSPITAL MARIO GARCIA
SOLUCIONES

1. B

2. C

3. A

4. C

5. C

HOSPITAL MARIO GARCIA
VOCABULARIO

1. **Médico**: Doctor
2. **Cirujano:** Surgeon
3. **Egresado:** A graduate
4. **Promoción:** Class
5. **Necesitados**: People in need
6. **Escasos recursos:** Scarce resources
7. **Graduación:** Graduation
8. **Puesto de trabajo**: Job
9. **Apenas**: Barely
10. **Habitantes:** Inhabitants
11. **Amables:** Friendly
12. **Cariñosas:** Affectionate
13. **Acogedoras:** Welcoming
14. **Agarra:** Grabs
15. **Uniformes médicos:** Medical uniforms
16. **Bata:** Lab coat
17. **Estetoscopio:** Stethoscope
18. **Otorrinolaringología**: Otorhinolaryngology
19. **Martillo**: Hammer
20. **Reflejos:** Reflexes
21. **Tensiómetro**: Blood pressure cuff
22. **Glucómetro:** Glucometer
23. **Bienvenida:** Welcome
24. **Horario:** Schedule
25. **Consulta:** Consultation
26. **Visita domiciliaria:** Home visit
27. **Trasladarse:** To move locations
28. **Discapacidad:** Disability
29. **Bata blanca:** White coat
30. **Consultorio:** Doctor's office
31. **Albañil**: Construction worker
32. **Dolor muscular:** Muscle pain
33. **Aumento**: Increase

34. **Temperatura corporal:** Body temperature
35. **Escalofríos**: Shaking chills
36. **Ojos:** Eyes
37. **Por casualidad**: By chance
38. **Prueba**: Test/exam
39. **Examin de Sangre**: Blood test/hematology
40. **Por mi cuenta:** On my own
41. **Resultados:** Results
42. **Puedo Ver:** I can see
43. **Infección:** Infection
44. **Síntomas:** Symptoms
45. **Proceso viral:** Viral process
46. **O sea que**: In other words
47. **Vigilar**: To look out
48. **Transcurso:** Passing (of time)
49. **Dolor abdominal:** Abdominal pain
50. **Síntoma:** Symptom
51. **Antigripal:** Anti-flu
52. **Chequeo:** Check
53. **Siguiente**: Following
54. **Embarazada:** Pregnant
55. **Prenatal:** Prenatal
56. **Pertinentes:** Pertinent
57. **Ecograma:** Ultrasound
58. **Examen de orina:** Urine test
59. **Edad gestacional**: Gestational age
60. **Evolución:** Evolution/Progress
61. **Infección urinaria**: Urinary infection
62. **Parto**: Birth
63. **Camilla:** Stretcher
64. **Examinarla:** Examine it
65. **Dispone**: To prepare
66. **Acostarse**: To lie down
67. **Creciendo**: Growing
68. **Barriga**: Belly
69. **Latidos**: Beats
70. **Bebé:** Baby
71. **Examen físico:** Physical exam
72. **Rutina:** Routine
73. **Chequeo:** Check
74. **Satisfecha:** Satisfied
75. **Descansar**: To rest
76. **Diagnósticos:** Diagnostics

77. **Señor mayor**: Old man
78. **Anciano**: Old man
79. **Cansado:** Tired
80. **Expectativas:** Expectations
81. **Ducha**: Shower
82. **Despertador:** Alarm clock
83. **Enfermeras:** Nurses
84. **Atenderlo:** Help him
85. **Comodidad:** Comfort
86. **Instrumentos:** Instruments
87. **Respirar**: To breathe
88. **Fiebre**: Fever
89. **Tos:** Cough
90. **Auscultar:** To listen to (medical examination)
91. **Pulmones:** Lungs
92. **Signos**: Signs
93. **Laboratorio:** Laboratory
94. **Neumonía:** Pneumonia
95. **Receta**: Prescription
96. **Antibióticos:** Antibiotics
97. **Reposo:** Rest
98. **Enfermedad:** Disease
99. **Tratamiento**: Treatment
100. **Al pie de la letra:** To the letter
101. **Gripe**: Flu
102. **Diario:** Daily
103. **Jocoso:** Humorous
104. **Disminuir:** To reduce
105. **Sanadora:** Healing
106. **Carrera**: Career
107. **Propósito:** Intention
108. **Apenado:** Embarrassed/Saddened
109. **Profesión:** Profession
110. **Pueblerinos**: Villagers
111. **Festejos**: Celebrations
112. **Remunerado:** Paid
113. **Inaguración:** Opening
114. **Cartel**: Sign

FANÁTICO #1
RESUMEN

Guillermo es un fanático del deporte, entusiasmo que
heredó de su padre. Está casado y tiene un hijo de diez años. Junto
a su esposa viven en Medellín, Colombia. Guillermo quiere que la
relación con su hijo sea igual a la que él tuvo con su padre con
respecto a los deportes, es por eso que comparten asistir a los
estadios y ver los juegos en vivo juntos. Un día, su hijo Enrique le
confiesa que quiere ser un gran jugador de baloncesto, por lo que
Guillermo lo apoya y se convierte en su fanático número uno.

*Guillermo is a sports fan, an enthusiasm that he inherited
from his father. He is married and has a 10-year-old son and lives
with his wife in Medellin, Colombia. Guillermo wants the
relationship with his son to be the same as the one he had with his
father in terms of sports, which is why they share attending
stadiums and watching live games together. One day, his son
Enrique confesses that he wants to be a great basketball player, so
Guillermo supports him and becomes his number one fan.*

FANÁTICO #1

Guillermo, quien vive en Colombia en la ciudad de
Medellín, es un **aficionado** de los deportes gracias a su padre que
siempre lo llevaba a ver los **partidos** de baloncesto, de **fútbol** y de
béisbol de su localidad.

Guillermo está casado y tiene un hijo varón de diez años de
edad, llamado Enrique, quien se ha interesado en el **baloncesto**,
específicamente desde hace seis meses.

1. **Aficionado**: Fan
2. **Partidos**: Matches
3. **Fútbol**: Soccer
4. **Béisbol**: Baseball
5. **Baloncesto:** Basketball

Debido a esto, Guillermo ha estado muy emocionado porque siempre ha deseado que a su hijo le gusten los deportes tanto como a él, para así poder **compartir** como compartió él con su papá.

La tarde del sábado **juega** el **equipo** de béisbol de su localidad **contra** el favorito de la **selección** colombiana. Guillermo quiere llevar al estadio a su hijo Enrique para que así pueda disfrutar del **partido** en vivo.

6. **Compartir**: Toshare
7. **Juega**: Plays
8. **Equipo:** Team
9. **Contra**: Against
10. **Selección:** Team
11. **Partido**: Match

Se dirigen hacia el **estadio**, compran las **entradas** que se ubican justo detrás de «Home». Estas entradas eran unas de las más **costosas**, pero con la característica de que se ven los **jugadores** de cerca y se aprecian todas las **jugadas**. Además, pueden interactuar con la mascota del equipo a **mitad** del partido.

12. **Estadio:** Stadium
13. **Entradas:** Tickets
14. **Costosas:** Costly

15. **Jugadores:** Players
16. **Jugadas:** Plays
17. **Mitad:** Half

Comienza el partido. Su hijo Enrique se ve muy **contento** y emocionado, siempre pendiente de **atajar** una **pelota** cuando un jugador de su equipo **bateaba** una **falta**.

En la **séptima entrada**, el bateador hace un swing y la pelota se dirige hacia arriba y hacia atrás. Al ver esto, Enrique se encuentra con su **guante** marrón totalmente **abierto** encima de su cara, esperando **capturar** la pelota, la cual llega a hacerlo sin ningún problema.

18. **Contento**: Happy
19. **Atajar**: To catch
20. **Pelota**: Ball
21. **Bateaba:** Was hitting
22. **Falta:** Foul
23. **Séptima:** Seventh
24. **Entrada:** Innings
25. **Guante:** Glove
26. **Abierto**: Open
27. **Capturar**: To capture

—Felicidades, hijo, has capturado tu primera pelota en el estadio, de seguro te llaman para tomarte una foto con la pelota y obtengas la **firma** del **bateador** —dice el papá emocionado por lo sucedido.

—¿Viste como he atrapado esa pelota, papá? Igual como lo hacen los profesionales en los juegos que pasan por los **canales** de televisión. ¿Será que lo **transmitieron** por **televisión** y mi mamá me pudo ver atrapar la pelota? —pregunta emocionado Enrique.

—No lo sé hijo, puede ser. Yo lo dije para que estuvieras pendiente del partido porque estábamos justo detrás de «Home» y allí **apuntan** las cámaras de televisión —dice Guillermo.

28. **Firma**: Signature (Autograph)
29. **Bateador:** Batter
30. **Canales**: Channels
31. **Transmitieron:** Transmitted
32. **Televisión**: TV
33. **Apuntan**: They point

Cuando termina esa entrada, ven a lo lejos a la **mascota** del equipo acercarse hacia ellos, una gran ave vestida con el **uniforme** local del equipo y un gran **bate** de **plástico**.

34. **Mascota**: Pet
35. **Uniforme**: Uniform
36. **Bate**: Bat
37. **Plástico:** Plastic

Llega hasta las **sillas** donde se encuentran Guillermo y Enrique y al estar cerca de ellos, la mascota del equipo saca una cámara y se toma una fotografía con ellos, la cual aparece en la **pantalla** gigante del estadio, para que todos la puedan ver.

Enrique se acerca a su padre corriendo con una sonrisa y emocionado por lo que acaba de pasar y ambos se quedan **disfrutando** de lo último que queda del juego de béisbol.

38. **Sillas**: Chairs

39. **Pantalla**: Screen

40. **Disfrutando:** Enjoying

Al día siguiente, Guillermo emocionado le cuenta todo lo que sucedió en el juego de béisbol a su esposa y le comenta que la semana **entrante** llevará a Enrique a disfrutar del partido **amistoso** de baloncesto entre la selección nacional de Colombia y la selección nacional de Estados Unidos.

Guillermo está muy ansioso por ver ese partido, ya que va a ver jugar a su jugador favorito de toda su vida, quien ha jugado desde siempre para el equipo favorito de Guillermo de la Asociación Nacional de Baloncesto Americano.

Enrique también está muy emocionado, porque el deporte que de verdad le gusta y le interesa es el baloncesto y siempre ha escuchado de la famosa selección de Estados Unidos y de sus increíbles jugadores.

41. **Entrante:** Upcoming

42. **Amistoso**: Friendly

Al llegar el día del partido, se dirigen a la **taquilla** para comprar las entradas.

Desafortunadamente, el señor encargado de la taquilla les informa que ya están totalmente **agotadas** y que no hay más **disponibles**.

Decepcionado por esa noticia Enrique y Guillermo se dirigen de nuevo a su vehículo para **retirarse**, pero en ese momento otro aficionado se les acerca y le dice:

—Tengo dos entradas para vender, no voy a poder disfrutar del partido por problemas personales y quiero que otras dos personas lo disfruten como yo lo hubiera hecho.

174

43. **Taquilla**: Ticket office

44. **Agotadas**: Sold out

45. **Disponibles:** Available

46. **Decepcionado:** Disappointed

47. **Retirarse:** Backing out

Emocionado por la noticia Guillermo se dispone a comprarle las dos entradas. Se dirigen corriendo a su respectiva puerta de entrada para ubicarse en sus **asientos**, ya que el partido estaba a punto de comenzar.

Cuando se sientan, ven a lo lejos al jugador estrella, quien recibe una **ovación** de pie cuando cruza las puertas.

48. **Asientos:** Seating

49. **Ovación**: Ovation

Entran a la **cancha** todos los jugadores de la selección de Estados Unidos y detrás de ellos camina entusiasmada y nerviosa, la selección de Colombia quienes también reciben una ovación de los **admiradores** colombianos que se encuentran en las sillas del estadio de baloncesto.

Durante todo el partido Guillermo no podía creer lo emocionado que se ve su hijo Enrique. En cada **canasta** se levanta a **celebrar** con **gritos** y **saltos** sin importar del equipo que sea la anotación.

50. **Cancha**: Court

51. **Admiradores:** Fans

52. **Canasta:** Basket

53. **Celebrar**: To celebrate

54. **Gritos**: Shouting

55. **Saltos**: Jumps

Al finalizar el segundo **tiempo** se presentan en la cancha dos **agrupaciones** musicales y luego de finalizar sus canciones se disponen a realizar un show muy animado junto al **público**.

El animador necesita de la participación de un **integrante** del público para **lanzar** el **balón** desde la mitad de la cancha. El participante tiene tres oportunidades de lanzar el balón y si lo logra se lleva dos entradas para los próximos cinco partidos amistosos que se realizarán en ese mes.

56. **Tiempo**: Time

57. **Agrupaciones:** Groupings

58. **Público:** Public

59. **Integrante:** Member

60. **Lanzar**: To throw

61. **Balón**: Ball

Al ver que empezaba el show, Enrique le pregunta a su padre:

—Papá, ¿crees que nos pueda tocar a nosotros?

—Vamos a ver, hijo. Tienes que estar **pendiente** del **número** que está en la parte de abajo de tu asiento y si dicen ese número por el **micrófono**, tienes la oportunidad de participar —dice Guillermo.

—Está bien, papá, vamos a **cruzar los dedos** para que digan mi número —dice emocionado Enrique.

62. **Pendiente:** Pending

63. **Número:** Number

64. **Micrófono:** Microphone

65. **Cruzar los dedos**: Cross fingers

Se escucha en todo el estadio la voz del **anfitrión**:

—Muy bien aficionados, ¡escuchen con atención! Voy a decir un número que lo tienen que ubicar **debajo** de sus asientos. La persona que tiene el número que digo, se **apresura** y baja hasta acá, a mi lado, para empezar la **prueba**.

Se escucha el **redoble** de los **tambores** que forman parte de la animación y se escuchan por todos los **altavoces** del estadio:

—Y el número es el... ¡502! —dice el anfitrión por el micrófono.

—Yo tengo el 202, no **gané**. ¿Qué número tienes?, hijo —pregunta Guillermo a Enrique.

—Yo tampoco gané papá, mi asiento es el 346 —dice Enrique decepcionado y emocionado a la vez por el partido.

66. **Anfitrión**: Host

67. **Debajo:** Below

68. **Apresura:** You hurry

69. **Prueba:** Proof

70. **Redoble:** Roll

71. **Tambores**: Drums

72. **Altavoces**: Speakers

73. **Gané**: I won

Al finalizar el partido, Guillermo logra hablar con el señor de **seguridad**, quien le deja pasar y tomar una foto con su hijo Enrique y su **ídolo**.

Al llegar a su casa, ambos comentan emocionados lo que había ocurrido en el partido de baloncesto.

Muy impresionada, la mamá de Enrique ve la foto que Guillermo y Enrique se pudieron tomar y no puede creer que finalmente **lograron** dos de sus sueños, ver jugar a su ídolo del baloncesto americano y también tomarse una foto para el recuerdo.

Al día siguiente Enrique le comenta a su papá que quiere **practicar** baloncesto hasta llegar a convertirse en un jugador profesional, para que así esté orgulloso de su hijo y en un futuro sea tan fanático de él como de cualquiera estrella.

74. **Seguridad:** Security
75. **Ídolo:** Idol
76. **Lograron:** They got
77. **Practicar:** To practice

Emocionado por esta noticia, Guillermo le comenta a Enrique que no importa lo que quiera lograr en su vida siempre y cuando lo haga con amor y **esfuerzo**. Y le dice:

—Sé que serás el mejor jugador de baloncesto del mundo, y a donde quiera que llegues en tu **carrera** como **deportista**, siempre seré tu fanático número uno.

78. **Esfuerzo:** Effort
79. **Carrera:** Career
80. **Deportista:** Athlete

Conmocionado por las palabras de su padre, Enrique se propone a practicar diariamente baloncesto para llegar a ser una gran **estrella**.

Pasan los años y Enrique logra entrar en la selección colombiana de baloncesto. Tras mucha práctica y esfuerzo y sobretodo mucho amor, logra ser uno de los **mejores** jugadores del equipo, nunca olvidando las palabras de su padre.

Guillermo, muy **orgulloso** de los **logros** de su hijo, no se pierde ningún partido, siempre sentado en la primera **fila** junto a su esposa, **alentándolo** con **pancartas**.

81. **Estrella:** Star
82. **Mejores**: Top
83. **Orgulloso**: Proud
84. **Logros**: Achievements
85. **Fila**: Row
86. **Alentándolo:** Encouraging him
87. **Pancartas:** Banners

Un día, en un partido muy importante para Enrique, como era de esperarse, Guillermo y su esposa están **sentados** en la primera fila del estadio.

Comienza el partido y Enrique anota el punto **decisivo** para el **triunfo** de su equipo sobre sus **contrincantes**.

88. **Sentados**: Seated
89. **Decisivo**: Decisive
90. **Triunfo**: Triumph
91. **Contrincantes:** Opponents

Y solo se escuchan los gritos de emoción de su padre Guillermo.

—¡Ese es mi hijo y estoy muy orgulloso de él! —grita Guillermo con emoción.

Luego de celebrar con su equipo, Enrique corre a donde se encuentran sus padres y ve que su papá tiene una camiseta muy linda que dice con enormes letras rojas «Fanático #1».

Enrique con sus ojos llenos de lágrimas, **agradece** a su papá por el **apoyo** y le dice:

—Gracias por llevarme a aquel juego de baloncesto donde conocimos a tu ídolo, si no es por ti, no estaría aquí.

—Ahora tú eres mi ídolo, hijo. ¿Me puedo tomar una foto contigo? —pregunta Guillermo entre risas.

Y como en todos los partidos, Guillermo y su esposa siempre ven a su hijo desde la primera fila del estadio.

92. **Agradece:** He thanks
93. **Apoyo:** Support

PREGUNTAS

1. **¿Cómo se llama el hijo de Guillermo?**
   a. José
   b. Jorge
   c. Enrique

2. **¿Cuál es el deporte del primer juego que ven Guillermo y Enrique en el estadio?**
   a. Fútbol
   b. Béisbol
   c. Baloncesto

3. **¿Cuál es el deporte que más le gusta e interesa a Enrique?**
   a. Baloncesto
   b. Fútbol
   c. Béisbol

4. **¿Dónde se sienta Guillermo para ver a su hijo jugar?**
   a. Detrás del «Home»
   b. En la primera fila
   c. No va a verlo

FANÁTICO #1
SOLUCIONES

1.C

2.B

3.A

4.B

FANÁTICO #1

VOCABULARIO

1. **Aficionado**: Fan
2. **Partidos**: Matches
3. **Fútbol**: Soccer
4. **Béisbol**: Baseball
5. **Baloncesto:** Basketball
6. **Compartir:** To share
7. **Juega**: Plays
8. **Equipo:** Team
9. **Contra**: Against
10. **Selección:** Team
11. **Partido**: Match
12. **Estadio:** Stadium
13. **Entradas:** Tickets
14. **Costosas:** Costly
15. **Jugadores:** Players
16. **Jugadas:** Plays
17. **Mitad:** Half
18. **Contento**: Happy
19. **Atajar**: To catch
20. **Pelota**: Ball
21. **Bateaba:** Was hitting
22. **Falta**: Foul
23. **Séptima**: Seventh
24. **Entrada:** Innings
25. **Guante**: Glove
26. **Abierto**: Open
27. **Capturar**: To capture
28. **Firma**: Signature (Autograph)
29. **Bateador:** Batter
30. **Canales**: Channels
31. **Transmitieron:** Transmitted
32. **Televisión**: TV
33. **Apuntan**: They point
34. **Mascota**: Pet
35. **Uniforme**: Uniform
36. **Bate**: Bat
37. **Plástico**: Plastic
38. **Sillas**: Chairs
39. **Pantalla**: Screen
40. **Disfrutando:** Enjoying
41. **Entrante:** Upcoming
42. **Amistoso**: Friendly
43. **Taquilla**: Ticket office
44. **Agotadas**: Sold out
45. **Disponibles**: Available
46. **Decepcionado:** Disappointed
47. **Retirarse:** Backing out
48. **Asientos**: Seats
49. **Ovación**: Ovation

50. **Cancha**: Court
51. **Admiradores:** Fans
52. **Canasta:** Basket
53. **Celebrar**: To celebrate
54. **Gritos**: Shouting
55. **Saltos**: Jumps
56. **Tiempo**: Time
57. **Agrupaciones:** Groupings
58. **Público:** Public
59. **Integrante:** Member
60. **Lanzar**: To throw
61. **Balón**: Ball
62. **Pendiente:** Pending
63. **Número**: Number
64. **Micrófono:** Microphone
65. **Cruzar los dedos**: Cross fingers
66. **Debajo:** Below
67. **Apresuran:** You hurry
68. **Anfitrión**: Host
69. **Prueba:** Proof
70. **Redoble:** Roll
71. **Tambores**: Drums
72. **Altavoces:** Speakers
73. **Gané**: I won
74. **Seguridad:** Security
75. **Ídolo**: Idol
76. **Lograron:** They got
77. **Practicar:** To practice
78. **Esfuerzo:** Effort
79. **Carrera:** Career
80. **Deportista:** Athlete
81. **Estrella:** Star
82. **Mejores**: Top
83. **Orgulloso**: Proud
84. **Logros**: Achievements
85. **Fila**: Row
86. **Alentándolo:** Encouraging him
87. **Pancartas:** Banners
88. **Sentados**: Seated
89. **Decisivo**: Decisive
90. **Triunfo**: Triumph
91. **Contrincantes:** Opponents

I hope you enjoyed this collection of short stories. A tremendous amount of effort went into its creation. If you like this book please do me a favor and leave a review. It will really help others recognize my work.

Made in the USA
Columbia, SC
24 April 2021